G. Race.

Great Sea Mysteries

Also available in this series

Aidan Chambers
Haunted Houses
More Haunted Houses
Great British Ghosts

Richard Garrett
Hoaxes and Swindles
True Tales of Detection
Narrow Squeaks!

Frank Hatherley
Bushrangers Bold!

Marie Herbert
Great Polar Adventures

Sorche Nic Leodhas
Scottish Ghosts

Carey Miller
Airships and Balloons
Submarines!

Nicholas Monsarrat
The Boys' Book of the Sea

Eric Williams
Great Air Battles

Piccolo True Adventures

GREAT SEA MYSTERIES

Cover illustration by George Underwood
Text illustrations by Edward Mortlemans

Richard Garrett

A Piccolo Original
Pan Books London and Sydney

First published 1971 by Pan Books Ltd,
Cavaye Place, London SW10 9PG
4th printing 1976

ISBN 0 330 02799 9

Made and printed in Great Britain by
Cox & Wyman Ltd, London, Reading and Fakenham

Contents

Sailors' Talk

Being a brief guide to some of the terms you may come across in this book

Binnacle: A stand on which the ship's compass is mounted.

Fo'c'sle: The word is really 'forecastle'. In the old warships it was a raised area up at the front, from which it was possible to shoot down on to the enemy's deck. Later on, it was enclosed, and became the place where the seamen usually lived.

Knots: The units indicating a ship's speed. The expression is an abbreviation for 'nautical miles per hour'. A nautical mile is longer than a statute mile: the distance is defined by the British Admiralty as 6,080 feet. Thus a ship travelling at 10 knots would be moving at approximately 13½ land miles per hour.

Mizzen: The third mast in a three-masted sailing ship (the other two were the foremast and the mainmast).

P & O: The Peninsular and Oriental Steam Navigation Company which, before the introduction of long-range air services, was the way in which most people travelled to or from India. It was from the P & O liners that the expression 'posh' came about. The initials stand for **P**ort **O**utwards, **S**tarboard **H**ome. Because of the prevailing winds when the ship was steaming through very hot weather, passengers were more comfortable if they had cabins on the port side on the voyage to India – on the starboard side when returning to Britain.

Poop: The aftermost part of a ship. In many vessels it is raised above the main deck in much the way in which the fo'c'sle is raised at the front.

Port: The left-hand side of a ship, looking towards the bows.

Quarterdeck: the area between the mizzenmast (or the aftermost mast) and the poop. It was the most exclusive part of the vessel, and it was here that the senior officers and the cabin-class passengers (i.e. those who paid the top prices) promenaded for their exercise.

Screw: A ship's propeller – so called because the early versions were shaped like the thread of an enormous screw.

Starboard: The right-hand side of a ship looking towards the bows.

Steerage: The part of the ship in which passengers travelled at the cheapest rate. It was usually in the afterpart above the rudder (hence, 'steerage'), though sometimes it was up front in the fo'c'sle.

Topgallant: On the main mast of a sailing ship, the lowest sail was called the 'main sail'. Above that there was the main topsail; and above that. . . . Well, how does one find a word which is more top than 'top'? They settled for 'topgallant', but their problems were still not over: They called the next one the 'main royal' and the final one the 'main skysail'.

Warning to Mariners

Readers are warned that most of the episodes described in this book took place before the days of wireless. The only signalling equipment on board the vessels were lamps and flags. Furthermore, all but a very few of the events happened before man had learnt to fly – let alone discovered the helicopter. For these reasons, many lives were lost and some ships vanished without trace. Nowadays, the toll of lives at sea is very much smaller, and the mysteries are far fewer.

The facts in these stories are as true as I can make them. I cannot pretend, however, that the spoken words are exactly what the characters said. There was, after all, no reporter there to take them down. Consequently, I have written what I think they would have said. The rest, with the exception of the *Flying Dutchman*, is entirely factual.

R. G.

Tunbridge Wells

I

Why Shoot the Skipper?

At 10.30 on a warm evening in August 1902, Captain Peattie, master of the sailing ship *Leicester Castle*, was lying on his bunk, composing himself for sleep. He was a tough but amiable man from Paisley in Scotland, and he liked to read a page or two before turning out his lamp. It helped him to relax.

The *Leicester Castle* was ghosting through the calm waters of the Pacific at a speed of three and a half knots. About 300 miles away to the south lay the Pitcairn Islands, where the *Bounty*'s mutineers had settled. But, at this moment, Captain Peattie's thoughts were far removed from the *Bounty*, or mutiny, or any of the hazards which, from time to time, have threatened the safety of men at sea.

The book was a good one. And, in any case, Captain Peattie had nothing to cause him any anxiety. Since they had sailed from San Francisco on passage to London, the going had been good. Right now, he wished there were more wind, but he had to admit that the calm, warm weather was very agreeable.

He was well pleased with his crew. There were eighteen of them in all, including three Americans who had signed on at San Francisco: a man named Hobbs from somewhere in the state of Illinois, an Idaho man named Ernest Sear, and James Turner from Portland, Oregon.

Hands in San Francisco were hard to come by, and it

was no secret that the town's boarding-house keepers worked a racket rather like the exploits of the press gang in the darker days of the Royal Navy.

They would feed a man liquor until he was unconscious, or else they would put dope in his food. Whichever the method, the end product was an unconscious individual, who would be carried to the gang-plank of a ship about to sail. In return for a small fee, he would be handed over to the mate and the boarding-house keeper would go back to replenish his stock of human merchandise.

By the time the unlucky man woke up, usually with a searing headache, the ship would be at sea and all escape impossible. Thus the mates recruited the missing members of their crews, and thus the boarding-house keepers amassed their wealth, and everybody was very happy except those who had been forced into a job of which they wanted no part.

Captain Peattie, who believed in letting his first mate do his work without unreasonable interference, was not sure by what means the three Americans had become part of his crew. It was quite possible that one – or, indeed, all – of them had come aboard in the arms of a dissolute boarding-house keeper. But, if this were so, the men seemed to have accepted their fate philosophically. All seamen grumble sometimes, but these men were no more trouble than anyone else. Indeed, they were quiet, hard-working, and Captain Peattie approved of them.

The captain turned over a page. The second mate, a twenty-four-year-old officer from Edinburgh named Nixon, was on watch. Nixon was a good man. Most reliable. You could leave things safely in his hands. If the calm weather continued, Captain Peattie could look forward to a good night's sleep.

He turned over another page. At that moment, however, his reading was interrupted by a soft tap on the door. It was hesitant, half-hearted, as if the visitor were nervous.

'Come in,' Captain Peattie called.

The door opened and the man named Sears from Idaho stood on the threshold.

'Yes, Sears?' the captain asked.

'I'm sorry to disturb you, Captain, sir,' Sears said. 'But could you come outside please?'

The man looked pale and worried, as if he had received some kind of shock. Captain Peattie put his book down.

'Why?' he asked. 'What seems to be the trouble?'

'A man's just fallen from one of the spars. Mr Nixon thinks he has broken a leg. He says can you examine him.'

On board a sailing ship, the captain was more than an able navigator and the leader of his crew. He had, when necessary, to be doctor and clergyman as well. If a man died at sea, it was the captain who read the funeral service. And, if a man and a woman on a passenger ship wished to become married, the captain was authorized to conduct the ceremony.

In the field of medicine, major surgery was obviously out of the question, but the captain was required to have a thorough knowledge of first-aid, and would think nothing of making a thoroughly professional job of setting a fracture.

'Very well, Sears,' Captain Peattie said. 'Tell Mr Nixon I'll be in the saloon.'

'Yes, sir,' the man said.

Captain Peattie climbed down from his bunk, pulled on a pair of trousers over his pyjamas, and picked up a box of matches.

The saloon was in darkness. He groped his way to the

table in the centre and, striking a match, lit the oil lamp. The steward had cleared away the evening meal some while ago, and there was nothing on the table apart from the lamp. By its light, he noticed that Sears was still standing in one of the two doors which led out on to the deck.

'Well – hurry, man,' Captain Peattie said. 'Ask Mr Nixon to bring the casualty down right away. We'll have him put on this table.'

To his surprise, Sears said nothing and made no movement towards the deck.

But now there was a sailor blocking the other door. It was Hobbs, the man from Illinois and the most silent of the three Americans.

Captain Peattie experienced a feeling of unease. The strange behaviour of Sears, who was still standing in the doorway, was one reason. The sudden appearance of Hobbs was another. But even more disquietening was the fact that the latter was holding a length of wood, which bore an uncomfortable likeness to a club.

'What is it?' Captain Peattie growled.

Hobbs said nothing. With a quick movement he threw the club to Sears and withdrew his right hand from a trouser pocket. It was gripping a revolver.

Captain Peattie advanced a pace and, at the same time, Hobbs squeezed the trigger. The explosion made a considerable din in the small saloon. The captain felt a hard blow just above his heart, and then a sharp, burning pain.

But he was far from dead. He leapt at Hobbs, who fired again. This time the bullet struck the captain in the arm. It threw him off balance, which enabled Hobbs to attack with the length of wood. He hit Captain Peattie several times over the head until he fell unconscious to the floor.

'Hobbs squeezed the trigger . . .'

He then fired two more shots. Again, they landed in one of the captain's arms.

The noise of the shooting had reached the ears of Nixon who was on the poop and, contrary to the tale told by Sears, was not busy ministering to an injured sailor. The young man ran to the door of the saloon to investigate. Hobbs swung round and squeezed the trigger again. This time his aim was all too accurate. The bullet went straight through the second mate's heart.

Others had been aroused by the explosions. The steward and a sailor named Denny were the first to enter the saloon. They found the captain bleeding and unconscious on the floor. Hobbs and Sears had vanished. The scene, as the steward said afterwards, 'was a shambles'.

The first mate was next on the scene. Fortunately one of the crew, a man named Brennan, had served in the Ambulance Corps in South Africa, and had gained experience in how to dress gunshot wounds. The mate put him in charge of the wounded captain, and ordered the rest of the hands to muster in the shelter of the poop.

Everyone was there – except the three Americans.

'Now look here,' the mate said. 'We have to accept the fact that there's an armed man aboard this ship. Indeed, there may be three of them. We can't see them in this darkness, but they might be able to pick us off one at a time. I want everyone to keep under cover until first light. Then we'll make a search.'

For the next two hours, they waited anxiously. But then, at half past midnight, a seaman spotted a curious object by the light of the starboard navigation light. It was a very rough-and-ready raft, which must have been launched from some point near the stern of the vessel, and on which were seated the three Americans. It floated past and very soon disappeared into the night. So far as anyone can tell, it was never seen again.

A search revealed that the Americans had taken all their personal belongings with them, plus a week's supply of food and water. The raft had been made by lashing some planks – each of them twelve feet long by four inches wide – to cork floats that had been removed from one of the lifeboats. In the vast, sometimes stormy, waters of the Pacific Ocean a week's supply of rations would have been more than enough. The raft would never have lasted that long.

Second mate Nixon was buried at sea next day. Captain Peattie, under the expert nursing of Brennan, recovered and presently assumed command of the ship once more. But, and Captain Peattie asked himself this question many times afterwards, what was it all about?

The three Americans had almost certainly been coerced aboard the ship by an unscrupulous boarding-house keeper back in San Francisco. No doubt they had a strong grudge against the ship and her officers. This was unfair: the boarding-house keeper was the man to blame, but he was several thousands of miles away, whilst these men were on the spot.

The revolver, it turned out, had been stolen (presumably by Hobbs) from Nixon. Quite possibly it was loaded with six rounds. The captain had stopped four of them, and Nixon had been killed by another. That left only one.

This may explain why they made off so quickly. If Hobbs had only one bullet left, they would have been helpless against the rest of the crew.

But why choose this particular moment for such an adventure? To attempt to murder the captain as an act of revenge may be understandable. To attempt to escape from a ship in which they had never wanted to serve may sound reasonable. But why make the attempt on a flimsy wooden raft, when the vessel was over 300 miles from the nearest land?

Admittedly, the weather was good, but that, in itself, was no reason at all. What is more likely is that they misheard the position of the ship. Somewhere along the line, somebody dropped a nought from the figure 300. They may have imagined that they were only thirty miles from the Pitcairn Islands – the home of those other mutineers. On such a night, they might have managed to cover this distance, even on such a botched-up contraption as their raft. But 300! It seems almost certain that the missing nought cost murderer Hobbs and his two friends their lives.

2

The Empty Ship

There was blue everywhere. The pale blue spread of the sky, decorated with wisps of white, like feathers torn from the tail of a swan. And the blue-black, gun-metal, ocean: rippled by the gentle northerly wind, and here and there spangled with light – as the small waves caught and flashed back the afternoon sun.

The time was two o'clock. Captain Morehouse walked backwards and forwards across the *Dei Gratia*'s narrow poop. Now and again, he teased the hair of his thick brown beard. Sometimes he glanced upwards at the white array of the brig's sails. They were making about four knots, which was not, perhaps, as fast as he would have liked.

But how could a man grumble? The winds had been favourable all the way from New York. It had been a good trip so far, and, within a day or so, they would have sailed out of the Atlantic and into the Mediterranean. It was now December 4th. By Christmas, they would be secured snugly alongside a quay, waiting for a new cargo, and with plenty of time in which to enjoy themselves.

He turned to the second mate, who was on watch beside the wheel.

'What's our position?' he asked.

'Thirty-eight twenty north, seventeen fifteen west, Skipper,' the man said. 'We're well to the north of Santa Maria.'

As if he hoped to see the island, which is the most south-easterly of the Azores group, the captain regarded the horizon. There was nothing on the sharp line which separated the dark blue sea from the light blue sky. Santa Maria was tucked away beneath it, invisible.

Captain Morehouse's eyes, as if setting off on a voyage, began to follow the line. And then, suddenly, they stopped.

'Hand me the glass please, mister,' he said.

The second mate passed him the telescope. For several moments, the captain regarded the smallest of specks, trying, as it were, to drag out the details from something which was too far away to have any identity.

He beckoned to the second mate. 'Come over here,' he said. 'Take a look.'

And, presently: 'What do you make of it?' 'It's a ship all right. A brigantine, I'd say.'

'Huh!' Captain Morehouse grunted his agreement.

Before very long, it became clear that the two vessels were drawing closer to each other. The black speck assumed shape and then, gradually, details. Unlike the *Dei Gratia*, she had only two sails set on the foremast, and there seemed to be something wrong with her rigging. Captain Morehouse was puzzled.

'Strange,' he muttered. And: 'Odd'. And: 'I don't seem to understand'.

'Looks as if she's had a rough passage,' the second mate offered.

'Yes – and then again, no. There's damage, I'll agree. But nothing which couldn't be put to rights. And then, do you know, I have the impression there's no one on deck. Look again through the glass, and see what you think.'

The second mate looked. 'No,' he said. 'Nobody on

deck. There's not even a man at the wheel. It's the oddest darned thing.'

Captain Morehouse beckoned to one of the sailors 'My compliments to Mr Deveau,' he said, 'and ask him to join us on deck.'

Mr Deveau was the first mate of the *Dei Gratia*. He had been on watch for a large part of the night, and now he was asleep in his cabin. But, as he emerged from the companionway and on to the poop, nobody would have guessed this. His eyes were alert and there was no suggestion of fatigue in his brisk walk.

'Something the matter, Skipper?' he asked.

'Nothing the matter – something peculiar. Take a look at that vessel over there.'

Mr Deveau looked and breathed a whistle of surprise. 'I guess there must be a crew on board,' he said with an uncertain smile, 'but they must be drunk. Nobody's sailing that ship. She's sailing herself.'

The captain gave a brief order to the helmsman. 'We'll get within hailing distance,' he said, 'and see whom we can rouse.'

As they drew closer, more details became apparent and most of them confirmed the earlier impressions. Something, most certainly, was wrong. At least two of the sails had obviously been blown away, and another was hanging from a stay in a manner that no sail made by man was ever intended to hang. The deck was deserted, and it looked as if the compass had been damaged.

'Get all men on deck,' Morehouse told the mate. And: 'Heave to!' He cupped his hands to his mouth, and called across the water: 'Ahoy there! Ahoy there!' There was no reply. The strange vessel continued, crablike on her uncertain course, unaware of everything around her.

'Something, most certainly, was wrong'

When all the sailors were assembled, Captain Morehouse again addressed the mate. 'Take Mr Wright and one other man. Lower the longboat and go over and board her. I'm not at all happy about what I see.' He paused and then smiled. 'Or maybe I am. It could be that we're about to make ourselves some money.'

'Salvage?' the mate asked.

'It's a possibility, mister,' the captain said. 'Get over there as fast as you can.'

The two mates and a seaman climbed into the boat. With a rattle of the running gear, the craft dropped the few feet from the deck to the sea. They unhitched her and got the oars out. With strong, smooth strokes, they rowed beneath the counter of the mysterious vessel's stern towards the far side. The name and port of registration were painted in bold white letters. She came, it seemed, from New York. Her name was *Mary Celeste*.

We must now go back to November 4th, 1872 – just over a month before Captain Morehouse had sighted the brigantine, and the two mates of the *Dei Gratia* had set off on their short trip in the longboat. It was a crisp day in early winter, with frost in the air, and the usual bustle of activity on Pier 30 in New York's East River. The *Mary Celeste* was loading a cargo of 1,700 casks of alcohol for Genoa. The first mate, Albert G. Richardson, was in charge of operations on deck.

Down in the saloon, the brigantine's master, Captain Benjamin Spooner Briggs, was studying the list of his crew. Among them were four German seamen. Three of them came from the Fresian Islands, and Captain Briggs knew them by reputation. They were quiet, steady men – good workers and not given to trouble-making. The fourth, Gottschalk, was unknown to him.

This was to be Captain Briggs' first voyage in the *Mary Celeste*. He was a man of thirty-seven, sturdily built and with a carefully trimmed black beard and moustache. Previously, he had commanded a schooner and then, briefly, a barque.

His present ship had originally been owned by a Nova Scotia firm, which had named her the *Amazon*. Now she belonged to a partnership of four people, in which Briggs owned eight of the twenty-four shares.

While Captain Briggs was doing his paper work, his wife, Sarah, was fussing over their two-year-old daughter, Sophia. A voyage to the Mediterranean in winter was something to be enjoyed, and Mrs Briggs was looking forward enormously to a few days in Genoa. She also hoped to bring a woman's sense of domestic orderliness to life in the *Mary Celeste*'s saloon. She had brought her sewing machine with her and, for the Briggs family was fond of music, a small organ – no bigger than an upright piano – called a melodian.

'It will be nice, Ben,' she had told her husband. 'We can have some songs on the trip, and that will pass the time.'

Captain Briggs had agreed that it would, indeed, be pleasant.

Now she said: 'It was good of Mr Richardson to have the melodian put on board so carefully. I declare there's not so much as a scratch on it.'

'Yes, yes, Sarah,' Captain Briggs muttered. He had other things on his mind. The *Mary Celeste* had just undergone a complete refit, which was all to the good, for she had been in bad shape when he took her over. But, even now, she was not complete. The melodian might have been loaded satisfactorily, but some lout of a docker had damaged the longboat. There was no time in which to carry out the necessary repairs, and it would have to be left behind.

This meant that the *Mary Celeste* would only have one boat on board for the trip – an eighteen-foot yawl, which was normally carried on davits across the stern.

Briggs hauled himself out of his chair and went on deck. 'All going OK, Bert?' he said to the mate.

'All going OK. I've told them to be especially careful of the alcohol. In a wooden ship like this, it could be dangerous. If it caught fire, there'd be nothing left of the *Mary Celeste*.'

'I know what you mean. Still, we should make a profit on this trip.'

Richardson, who was related to the firm's senior partner by marriage, saw the sense of this.

'I'm going to stow the yawl on top of the main hatch,' he said. 'Does that suit you?'

'That'll be fine,' Captain Briggs said.

By the following day, the vessel was ready for sea. The hatches had been carefully battened down, the yawl was lashed in position. Escorted by a tug, the *Mary Celeste* edged away from the pier, and drifted down river on the tide to Staten Island. From his position in the stern, Captain Briggs looked with dislike at the lowering November sky. The water round about was being torn up into white tatters by a strong head wind.

'No good trying to sail against this, Bert,' he said to the mate. 'We'd be wasting our time and getting extremely uncomfortable into the bargain. Have them drop the anchor. We'll wait until the wind changes.'

They had to wait for two days, but the time passed pleasantly enough. In the evening, Mrs Briggs played her melodian, and one of the German seamen taught her some of the songs they sing in the Fresian Islands.

When, on the morning of November 7th, Captain Briggs came up on deck, he found things much more to his liking. The wind had backed round to the west, which was where it should have been in the first place.

'All hands on deck,' he told the mate. 'Let's get some sail on her. The sooner we're under way, the sooner we'll make Genoa.'

The seamen worked quickly. The great fields of white canvas unfolded. With a succession of jerks, the ropes stretched tight. The sails filled; a dribble of white foam at

Mary Celeste's bow became a triumphant plume. Gathering speed rapidly, the small sailing ship headed south-eastwards on course for the Azores, Cape St Vincent, Gibraltar, and thence to Genoa.

'If it stays like this, we'll make good time,' Captain Briggs remarked.

For the next seventeen days, the moody and cruelly impartial fates, which govern the lives of men at sea, were well disposed to the *Mary Celeste* and her crew. On November 24th, they sighted the Azores after no incidents. But Captain Briggs was not happy.

'I don't like the look of the glass, Bert,' he told the mate.

His companion shook his head. 'I know,' he said. 'It's falling fast.'

If the mercury in the barometer was falling, the wind was doing the opposite. By nightfall, it had worked itself up into a moderate gale. The sky was dark, with sheets of rain hammering the deck, and the ocean built itself up from a series of small hummocks into hills, and then into mountains.

Mary Celeste was flying along at nine knots, but this could not be allowed to continue. With such a high wind pressing itself against the sails, something, eventually, would break. The sails themselves might be torn away, or it could be worse. Ships had sometimes had their masts snapped into pieces by gales, and Captain Briggs was afraid this might happen to the *Mary Celeste*.

'Lower the main and take in the royals and top-gallants,' he yelled to the mate. By 'royals' and 'top-gallants', he was referring to the square sails at the head of the foremast.

'Come on, lads – lively now,' Mr Richardson called. The crewmen scrambled up the mast, cutting their hands on the wet rigging which was stretched tight and seemed as hard as steel. They got the sails in and regained the deck.

Throughout the night, Captain Briggs remained on deck. His wife brought him cups of coffee and, on each visit, she nervously asked: 'Will it be all right, Ben?'

'Sure it'll be all right,' her husband said. 'How's Sophia?'

The little girl, improbably enough, was fast asleep.

In his heart, Captain Briggs was less happy. As if the wind and the rain, and the wild bucking of the *Mary Celeste* as she fought the big seas – as if these were not enough, there was another hazard. Somewhere ahead of them was the island of Santa Maria, a lonely chunk of rock-fringed land in the middle of the ocean, with no lighthouses to warn mariners that it was there.

The thick overcast of the storm made it impossible to check their position by the stars. Captain Briggs could do nothing more than hope that his dead reckoning was right, and that they were a safe distance away from the island.

At five o'clock in the morning, the wind dropped a little, and a white, watery sun did its best to pierce the clouds in the east. In the grey half-light, Richardson was studying the horizon ahead through his telescope.

Suddenly he cried: 'There she is – dead ahead.'

He pointed to a smudge of land about fifteen miles away.

'Steer north-east by north,' Captain Briggs snapped the change of course to the helmsman. Then: 'Where's that damned coffee?' His eyes were edged with red, and his face, pale after the long night of discomfort and anxiety, was deeply etched with dark lines.

'North-east by north it is,' the helmsman acknowledged.

Later, they had breakfast; and, at eight o'clock, Richardson took a bearing on Santa Maria, which was now abeam. 'Eastern point bears SSW, 6 miles distant,' he noted in the log.

It was the final entry. From that moment onwards, nothing more is known of what happened on board the *Mary Celeste*, nor of what befell the crew, Mrs Briggs and the small girl who were aboard her.

The longboat from the *Dei Gratia* came alongside the brigantine. The seaman clambered up on deck and made a rope fast. The two mates followed him.

Deveau called again: 'Ahoy, *Mary Celeste* – who's on board?' But there was no answer.

'We'd better have a look round,' he told the others.

As they had expected, two sails had been blown away. The fore royal and the fore topgallant were neatly furled, but two of the other sails were missing, and a third had broken loose. The rigging was fouled up. The compass had been knocked from its position on top of the cabin, and was lying smashed on the deck. One of the hatch-covers had been blown off, and the ship's boat was missing.

'Quite a mess,' Deveau said. 'Let's take a look below.'

They searched every corner of the *Mary Celeste* and could not find a living soul on board her. The cabin skylight was raised, and this had let the water in. A clock on the bulkhead had stopped, and the captain's bed was unmade. Everywhere there was the feel and smell of moisture.

The hatch over the galley had been removed, and there was a foot of water inside. But this was as far as the chaos went. The pots and pans had all been washed up and put away in their correct places. This may have been a sign of the houseproud influence of Mrs Briggs – though, if it was, it seems strange that her husband's bed had not been made.

Deveau and his companions returned to the deck. By one of the hatches, they found a sounding rod, which suggested that someone had been measuring the depth of water in the hold. To satisfy himself, Deveau used the rod himself, and found that it amounted to just over three feet. For a wooden hull, which is bound to let a certain amount in and has to be pumped out daily, this was not bad. Certainly it was not sufficient to cause any captain in his right mind to abandon ship.

And yet that, to judge by the absence of anyone on board and the missing boat, was what must have happened. Deveau clambered down into the hold to examine the cargo. It was all in good order and properly stowed.

'I just can't make it out,' he said. 'Can you see anything I've missed?' he asked the second mate.

But that gentleman could only answer 'No'.

'Right – let's get back to our own ship.'

Captain Morehouse listened attentively to his officers' reports. 'We'll take her into Gibraltar,' he said. 'You, Mr Deveau – take seamen Anderson and Lund with you. Get over there and make everything shipshape. We'll stay by you. Let us know when you're ready to make sail.'

It took three hours to clear the accumulation of water, and two days to repair the rigging and get sail on her. On December 13th, after a trip in which there was no trouble, and in which no more clues had come to light, Gibraltar was sighted. A few hours later, the two ships anchored in the harbour.

The British authorities took over the *Mary Celeste*, and

informed Captain Morehouse that he and his crew must remain on hand until the mystery of this strange ship had been cleared up. Fortunately, they relented later on; for, otherwise, these reluctant guests would have been there for the rest of their lives. The mystery of the *Mary Celeste* was *never* cleared up.

Naturally, there was an inquiry. Deveau, who was the chief witness, was cross-examined over and over again.

No – he had no idea how the water had got into the galley. Yes – it was surprising that the skylight over the cabin had been left open. No – he had seen no signs of anything which might have suggested that any violence had taken place.

'I would like to remind you of this weapon,' the counsel for the British Government said. And here he held up an old sword which had been found in Captain Briggs' cabin. There were stains on the blade. 'Think carefully, Mr Deveau – does this not suggest violence?'

'I saw no signs of anything like that,' the mate said. He was telling the truth. When the sword was examined more carefully, it transpired that the stains were not caused by blood.

'Was there any evidence of a fire, or an explosion, having taken place? Remember – her cargo was alcohol.'

'There was no such evidence.'

The Surveyor of Shipping examined the brigantine, and his report was much the same as Deveau's. There seemed to be no good reason why the fore hatch and the galley hatch should have been forced off, and nothing to account for the smashed compass. Nor was there any suggestion that, after the rough night which they had endured before Richardson made the last entry in the log, the weather had worsened. In fact, it had improved.

Every trail of investigation led to a dead end. As Horatio Sprague, the United States Consul in Gibraltar at the time, was forced to tell his Government, there was absolutely no explanation why the crew should have abandoned an apparently sound ship in perfectly reasonable weather.

The search for a solution to the mystery of the *Mary Celeste* did not end with the adjournment of the court of inquiry. On and off ever since, men of imagination have been trying to work out an answer. They have ranged from the somewhat far-fetched idea that the whole thing was a figment of the imagination, a complicated confidence trick, and that the *Mary Celeste*, as such, never existed at all. This was no doubt based upon the fact that there was some technical irregularity about the way in which the ship was registered. It is ingenious, but is hardly worth serious attention.

There was a theory that, no matter what the stains on the sword blade might suggest to the contrary, there really had been violence on board – that the sailors had mutinied, slaughtered the officers and Captain Briggs' wife and daughter, and then made off in the boat. But, if this was so, they must have been very tidy mutineers, for they left everything in perfect order.

Just before the First World War, some papers turned up in North London. They belonged to a man who claimed to be the sole survivor of the *Mary Celeste*. His name had never been entered on the crew manifesto for the simple reason that, although he had travelled with the consent of Captain Briggs, he had, to all other intents and purposes, been a stowaway.

According to his story, Briggs had attempted to swim round the ship fully clothed. Others had joined him in the water, while the rest of the crew had watched from a small atform that had been rigged up as a playground for the Briggs' daughter. The platform gave way under their combined weight; they all fell into the water and were presently eaten by sharks. By some miracle, the spinner of this improbable yarn had clung on to a piece of timber and, a good few days later, had been washed up on the coast of North Africa.

Less fantastic were theories that the seepage of alcohol from the barrels had caused Captain Briggs to fear an imminent explosion; that he had expected his ship to go aground on the rocks of Santa Maria; and that the ship had been hit by a water spout, which might very well have ripped off the hatches and have accounted for the water in the hold and the galley.

Certainly, the measuring rod suggests that Captain Briggs had been worried about the amount of water on board. Perhaps he overestimated the peril from this source, and believed that his vessel was in immediate danger of foundering. In which case, he might have ordered the ship to be abandoned.

But then, in the boat, he and his companions must have seen that, in fact, there had been no peril at all. And, as they struggled to return to her, a puff of wind must have filled the brigantine's sails. And as they worked frantically to catch up, they must have seen their one hope of rescue sailing, unattended, beyond their reach.

That must have been the awful irony of the unsolved mystery of the *Mary Celeste*; for the boat in which, presumably, they misguidedly sought safety, turned out to be their coffin. No signs of it were ever found. The crew of the *Mary Celeste* certainly died at sea. The reason will never be known.

3

Whatever Became of the Waratah?

Mr Claude Sawyer, a passenger on the SS *Waratah* bound from Sydney to London via Durban and Cape Town, was, on his own admission, a nervous man. The voyage across the Indian Ocean had been attended by a good deal of bad weather. The *Waratah*, which was the latest addition to the Blue Anchor Line's fleet, had seemed to respond badly to such conditions.

One evening before dinner, Mr Sawyer had lain in his bath, watching the antics of the water. It appeared to him as if he and (for it followed) the ship were stationary, whilst the water was rolling from side to side. The experience was a trifle uncanny for Mr Sawyer realized that precisely the opposite was true. He also understood that the strange behaviour of the liquid was trying to tell him something.

By a small feat of observation and mathematics, he presently worked out what the message was. Unless he was very much mistaken, the ship was, at the extremity of each roll, heeling over at an angle of forty-five degrees.

Over a glass of sherry before going into the dining saloon Mr Sawyer discussed this phenomenon with a solicitor with whom he had struck up an acquaintance. Before studying law it seemed that this gentleman had served at sea. The combination of ocean-going experience and a legal mind made him an ideal recipient for Mr

Sawyer's doubts about the vessel on which their lives depended.

If he had expected any comfort, he was to be disappointed. The lawyer said that, yes, there did appear to be something a little bit odd about the *Waratah*'s behaviour in high seas. 'I've noticed,' he said, 'that she seems to be rather slow in recovering herself when she's pitching. It's almost as if she's a lazy ship.'

As the voyage continued, the weather improved, and Mr Sawyer, who was due to disembark at Cape Town, forgot all about his fears. But then, on the night before they reached Durban, he underwent an experience which brought the whole business back most vividly.

It must have been a nightmare, but it seemed so real that he could believe he was wide awake. Standing at the end of his bunk was a man wearing some kind of fancy-dress. In one hand he carried a large sword which was pointing with uncomfortable precision at Mr Sawyer. In the other, which he held above his head, there was a rag soaked with blood.

Terrified, Mr Sawyer woke up. Presently, his fear calmed for the time being, he fell off to sleep again. Once again the dreadful apparition appeared, and, once again, he woke up trembling. The dream occurred three times that night. Each time it was precisely the same in every detail. It was a rather limp and nervous Mr Sawyer who came down to breakfast that morning. And, of everyone on board the *Waratah*, there cannot have been anyone who greeted the arrival of Durban with more relief.

For Mr Sawyer's mind was made up. The message of the nightmare was obviously intended to be considered in the light of the bathwater episode and his conversation with the solicitor. Other people might do as they liked, but he intended to disembark at Durban, send a telegram to his wife, and make the rest of the trip in a Union Castle boat.

The telegram which he presently dispatched was short and explicit. 'Thought *Waratah* top heavy,' he wrote. 'Landed Durban. Love Claude.' No doubt Mr Sawyer's experience of nightmares was greater than his knowledge of naval architecture. Nevertheless, his telegram revealed a remarkable degree of intuition. One might, indeed, have wondered what was so special about Mr Sawyer that, out of the 93 passengers and the 119 crew members on board the *Waratah* at that time, he was the one to be singled out for survival.

The *Waratah* was a passenger-cargo steamer of 16,800 tons. She had been built on the Clyde, and had successfully completed her trials in October 1908. Afterwards she was handed over to her owners, the Blue Anchor Line, for service between the Australian ports, South Africa and London.

Her commander was Captain Ilbery, an experienced mariner who had been with the Blue Anchor Line ever since 1868, and who was the senior captain in the fleet. After the *Waratah*'s maiden voyage, Captain Ilbery said he was pleased with his new ship, though he did remark that she was difficult to handle in the intricate manoeuvres of going in and out of harbour.

It was also reported, some time afterwards, that he had observed the new ship was not so stable in rough weather as her sister, the *Geelong*. But this was never substantiated. Indeed, it was a strange thing that, contrary to custom, the *Waratah*'s owners never insisted upon a written report from her captain after that first trip – and that Captain Ilbery, on his own initiative, never wrote one. Had he done so, and if he had forced himself to consider every detail of his new charge's behaviour, a good many lives might have been saved.

Waratah left London for her second voyage on April 27th, 1909. After visiting Adelaide and Sydney, she reached Durban on July 25th. She remained in port for twenty-four hours and then, minus Mr Sawyer, she departed for Cape Town.

A few hours earlier, an elderly cargo vessel named the *Clan MacIntyre* had also sailed from Durban *en route* for Cape Town. But the *Waratah* was a good deal faster. At six o'clock on the morning of July 27th she overhauled the veteran freighter. The two ships exchanged messages by flashing their signal lamps.

'What ship?' asked *Clan MacIntyre*. '*Waratah* – for London,' came the reply. '*Clan MacIntyre*, for London. What weather did you have from Australia?' 'Strong south-westerly to southerly winds.' 'Thanks. Goodbye. Pleasant voyage.' 'Thanks,' signalled the *Waratah*. 'Same to you. Goodbye.'

As the men on the bridge of the *Clan MacIntyre* watched the large steamer pulling away from them until she vanished out of sight, they shared none of Mr Sawyer's misgivings. It never occurred to them that anything was wrong with the Blue Anchor Line's flagship, and yet there must have been. For that was the last that anyone ever saw of her. As she steamed down the coast of South Africa, the *Waratah* was sailing out of the world.

The story so far has been composed entirely of the facts. From this point onwards we are in waters which are just as confused as those through which *Waratah* travelled during her last hours. The only certain thing is that this part of the ocean is notorious for local storms which come hurtling in suddenly from the east. The weather that day worsened until, during the night, a gale was blowing at the full frenzy of its lungs. Other ships reported this, and the *Waratah* must have caught the full impact of it.

But what is one to make of the story told by the captain of a small steamer named the *Harlow*, which was in the vicinity of the *Waratah*'s estimated position at six o'clock on the evening of the 27th – twelve hours after she had exchanged greetings with the *Clan MacIntyre*? This gentleman reported having seen the smoke of a ship on the horizon. At first he thought the vessel was on fire, but then he dismissed the idea and went into the chart room.

Later, one of the crew reported the navigation lights of a ship about ten or twelve miles astern. The vessel was, he said, overtaking them rapidly. The captain nodded, completed his calculations, and walked out on to the wing of the bridge. There were no signs at all of any ship, but, as he looked aft, he noticed two bright flashes of light on the landward side.

'What do you reckon to that?' he asked the mate. 'They looked like explosions to me.'

'I don't believe they were,' the mate said. 'More likely bush fires ashore.'

Could they have been explosions on board the *Waratah*? Or were they, as the mate suggested, bush fires? The general opinion was that the mate was correct.

And what is one to make of the report from the Union Castle ship, *Guelph*, which, in some ways, is even more unsatisfactory? Three hours after the captain of the *Harlow* had seen whatever it was he saw, the *Guelph* sighted the lights of what seemed to be a large passenger ship five miles away. The two vessels exchanged signals. The *Guelph* flashed her name to the other ship, which replied. Unfortunately the visibility was bad, and the third officer, who was in charge of the exchange, could only make out the last three letters of her name – TAH.

That, you might say, should prove conclusively that they had sighted the *Waratah*. After all, to find two large passenger liners on the same route at about the same time, and the names of both ending in TAH, that, surely, would be too much of a coincidence.

Unfortunately, mathematics do not give strength to this idea. The position at which the *Guelph* sighted the stranger was only seventy miles south of the point at which the *Waratah* is known to have been in contact with the *Clan MacIntyre*. And yet, fifteen and a half hours had elapsed. With a service speed of thirteen knots, the *Waratah* ought to have covered well over 200 miles in this period.

Perhaps she had experienced trouble with her engines. But, if this were so, why hadn't the *Clan MacIntyre*, which was plodding along on the same course, overhauled her?

To bring further confusion to our story (for we can hope for little else in these dark waters) let us consider the account given several days later, when the steamer *Tottenham* came into port. The third officer claimed that he had seen human bodies floating in the sea. His assertion was supported by an apprentice who said that he had seen a little girl in a red dressing-gown. The second officer went along with the apprentice's story, except that he produced more detail. She was, he recalled, wearing a red cape and hood and black stockings. 'I put her age at between ten and twelve,' he said.

He also announced that he had seen a ship's bunk drift by.

Captain Cox, the master of the *Tottenham*, turned his ship round, and went back to investigate his officers' reports. When he reached the area in which the bodies were supposed to have been, he noticed that there were a number of sunfish and skates swimming close to the surface. And the chief engineer pointed to a large roll of newsprint with a red wrapper around it, which had been washed overboard from a freighter.

'There's your little girl,' he said.

But this was not the end of alleged sightings of human bodies. When the steamer *Insizwa* passed through the same area as that in which the *Tottenham*'s crew had either seen sunfish or corpses, a young girl or a roll of newsprint, the captain was certain that he saw victims of the *Waratah*. There were, he told a reporter when he docked at Cape Town, 'two in white clothes and two in dark clothes'. There was also an uncommonly large number of seabirds in the vicinity.

'But why,' asked the reporter, 'did you not lower a boat to recover them?'

'For one thing,' the captain explained, 'I had a number of ladies on board, and I didn't want to alarm them. For another, my cargo had shifted during the storm. The ship had a slight list and I considered that it would have been dangerous to heave to with such a heavy sea running.'

So they saw bodies, or they did not see bodies. The cold light of fact, which must never depend upon the imagination, shows that no bodies, no bunks, nothing at all, large or small, animate or inanimate was ever recorded from the *Waratah*. Assuming she sank, it was totally without trace.

On land the stories were no more helpful. Some days after the disappearance of the ship a man was found wandering about the countryside not far from the coast. He carried no means of identification; and, when questioned, he told the authorities that he was a survivor from the *Waratah*. After still more questioning it was established beyond any reasonable doubt that he was insane, and he was escorted to the local lunatic asylum.

Perhaps a little bit more believable is the story of an old man who inhabited a hut at the mouth of one of the rivers which pour themselves into the Indian Ocean along this stretch of coast. On the night of the storm, he said, he had been sitting outside watching the violence of the sea, and the huge waves which were crashing down on the rocks beneath him and throwing veils of white spray up into the

'. . . amid the fury which was raging below, he saw a large steamer . . .'

air. Suddenly, amid the fury which was raging below, he saw a large steamer travelling close inshore. He ran into his hut to pick up his night glasses for a closer inspection.

But, when he returned to the cliff-top, the ship had vanished.

True or false? Accurate reporting or an exercise of the imagination? We shall never know – except that it seems unlikely that the *Waratah* would have been quite so close to the shore at this point.

What, then, out of all this hotchpotch of fact and fantasy can be depended upon? The answer is 'nothing'. We may like to believe some of the stories, and we may prefer to disbelieve others, but none of them has anything to support them. Nor is any material evidence forthcoming. After the disappearance of the *Waratah*, three warships provided by the Australian Government searched the area for a month, and steamed over 2,700 miles. They found nothing. And nor did the *Sabina*, a vessel chartered by the Blue Anchor Line, which cruised for 83 days and covered 14,000 miles.

Was the *Waratah* an unstable ship? By comparison with the *Geelong*, the answer seems to be 'yes'. But that is only relative. Because ship B is less well behaved in rough seas than ship A, it does not necessarily follow that ship B will capsize. Still – it is something to work on.

Whether Mr Sawyer's bath-tub observations would amount to much in a court of law may be doubtful – though, possibly, some reliance might be put on the opinion of his lawyer friend. Certainly the *Waratah* ran into a very heavy storm after exchanging signals with the *Clan MacIntyre*. Quite possibly she was attacked by a particularly large wave and, before she could recover from its impact (remember that the solicitor called her a lazy ship), another exceptionally big one hit her. If she was poor in terms of stability, the second onslaught may very well have caused her to capsize. The lack of bodies may be explained by the sharks which infest this area, but there remains one fact for which no reasonable explanation has ever been ventured.

If the *Waratah* capsized, and *if* she plunged to the bottom of the Indian Ocean, why was none of the debris, which marks the graves of doomed ships, ever discovered? Sharks do not eat lifebuoys, or lifeboats, or oars, or deck-chairs, or anything else of this nature. We can assume that everything inside the ship went down with her, but there are innumerable loose, or potentially loose, objects on deck, and no traces of *them* were ever reported.

When the *Waratah* plunged into the depths of the Indian Ocean on that wild day in 1909, a great many secrets went with her.

4

A Coil of Serpents

The trouble with history is that it has a tiresome habit of leaving out the details. We know, for example, that King Charles I was executed, and we know the date on which this took place. Some people may even know, or *think* they know, what he thought on that grim morning. But who can tell us what he had for breakfast?

Similarly, King Henry V won the Battle of Agincourt (and several others). He wore armour: no doubt about that. But what did he wear underneath it? If the royal underwear was made of wool, it no doubt protected his skin against those clanking metal plates – but, surely, it would have been terribly hot?

In terms of small, personal facts, history is a flop.

Take the case of that June day in 1808, when a clergyman named Maclean was out in a boat off Coll. Coll is a small lozenge of land, one of many which litter the sea off the West Coast of Scotland. It is several miles south of the Isle of Eigg where Mr Maclean had his parsonage.

There were thirteen other boats in the vicinity, and there is little doubt about what their owners were up to. They were fishing. But what was Mr Maclean doing? Keeping an eye on his parishioners, perhaps? Or simply enjoying the sunshine of early summer? Or spinning a line for mackerel? The records say nothing about this, and it would be interesting to know the answer. For, if Mr

Maclean *was* fishing, he narrowly missed making the strangest catch that anyone had ever caught.

Or, it might be argued, a most amazing inhabitant of the sea just missed catching Mr Maclean.

The minister was not far from the shore, when he noticed what, at first, he thought was a rock. For want of anything better to do (which seems to suggest that he was *not* fishing), he rowed closer. It certainly looked like a rock, and Mr Maclean was about to dismiss it from his thoughts. He dipped his oars into the water and was on the point of taking his boat elsewhere, when a movement attracted his attention. To his astonishment, and then to his terror, the 'rock' began to raise itself up out of the water.

This was no insignificant chunk of granite: it was a horrible, broad, oval-shaped head, with two fearsome yellow eyes which were regarding him with more than casual interest. It was mounted on a thick, sinewy neck; and, beneath the neck, there was a pair of broad, brown, rough-skinned shoulders.

Mr Maclean did not wait to inspect the creature in any more detail. He pulled towards the island of Coll as if the furies of hell were on his tail, which, so far as this devout man could tell, was exactly where they were.

Some minutes later, breathless and considerably afraid, he reached the shelter of a small creek. He hauled his boat out of the water and stood, watching, on the sand. Meanwhile, the men in the other thirteen boats were also making for Coll and so, to everyone's dismay, was the monster.

As a matter of fact, it cannot have been quite such a fury as they imagined; for it passed close to one of the boats, and made no attempt to attack it.

Afterwards they were all agreed that it was between seventy and eighty feet long. Its body tapered to a tail at

'. . . a horrible, broad, oval-shaped head, with two fearsome yellow eyes . . .'

the far end; it had no fins; kept itself low in the water, and moved by undulating up and down.

The whatever-it-was followed the minister up the creek; took one more look at him; and then swam away. Its curiosity was very nearly its undoing, for the inlet was narrow, and it was not without a certain amount of difficulty that the strange intruder regained the open sea.

Seven years after the remarkable experience of Mr Maclean a similar creature was seen off the coast of Massachusetts in North America. Acting on the assumption that anything which has not been seen before *must* be hostile, and should therefore be killed, a local sportsman set off in a boat with his gun. He discharged two barrels of shot at the visitor. Either his marksmanship was in bad shape that day, or else the monster's skin was so tough that the tiny missiles just bounced off. At all events it dived down into the sea, apparently uninjured. The sportsman returned to shore with no new trophy to hang upon his wall.

For the next few years there were several sightings of sea serpents off the coast of North America. They were all similar to the creature seen off Coll, and they ceased to be regarded with any misgivings. Certainly, they seemed to be much more amiable than the brute which, a century or so earlier, had attacked a sailing ship which was on passage across the Atlantic.

The vessel was becalmed at the time, and the captain had ordered three men to paint the sides of the hull. They were working on a plank which was suspended from the deck on a couple of ropes. Suddenly, there was a flurry in the water beneath them and a huge creature, like an enormous octopus, appeared. Stretching out a giant arm, it wrenched two of the men off their perch and then returned to attack the third.

Clinging on to the side of the ship, he yelled for help. Other sailors appeared on deck. Armed with axes, they hacked away at the deadly arm and presently chopped it off. The monster seemed ready to have another go, and the seamen returned to the offensive with harpoons. By this time, the terrified sailor was safely on deck. His companions were obviously not causing the brute even mild discomfort, but it may have considered two men were a reasonable harvest for the day. At any rate, taking its prey with it, it swam off.

The third man became delirious and died that night. It was hardly surprising, for the monster's arm was twenty-five feet long, as thick as a tree trunk, and had suckers on it the size of saucepan lids. It was enough to drive anyone out of his mind.

We now move forward in time to the year 1848 and the month of July. The sky was overcast and the warship HMS *Daedalus* was rolling in the long, oily ocean swell. The commanding officer, Captain McQuhae, was on deck, when he noticed an object sticking out of the water. At first he thought it was a piece of wreckage, but then he observed that it was swimming towards them.

As it drew closer, he and his crewmen could see that it was some sort of sea monster. A dark brown head, with a patch of white at the neck, was extended about four feet out of the water. So far, it was very like Mr Maclean's monster, but this one differed from the other in one remarkable way. According to all the observers, the back of its head sprouted a thick mane – just like that of a horse. For a few minutes, it seemed to study the ship, and then it vanished.

If this really was a sea serpent, this particular spot in the Atlantic must have been its stamping ground. Later that year, a brig from the United States was lying alongside another vessel named the *Mary Ann*. The *Mary Ann* was handing over a consignment of mail, which the other ship was to deliver when she reached Boston.

They were very close to the position from which HMS *Daedalus* had sighted the monster, when, up from the mysterious deep, came a huge creature about, the observers reckoned, one hundred feet long. Its head, and the thick mane at the back, corresponded very closely with Captain McQuhae's description. Fortunately, or so they thought, the American brig had a gun on board. They packed it with an assortment of nails and iron scrap, and blasted off at the monster. The unfortunate creature reared its head out of the water and then plunged down into the sea.

'I think we've wounded it,' somebody said.

A boat was lowered. Before they could reach the swirling patch of sea, however, the monster reappeared, took one look at the unfriendly vessel, and then swam off at an estimated speed of between fifteen and sixteen knots.

Sailors, like anyone else, occasionally enjoy telling tall stories. Other sailors (also like anyone else) enjoy demolishing these fantasies. When, in December of the same year, Captain Smith of the *Peking* was about forty miles from the point at which his colleague, Captain McQuhae, claimed to have seen the sea serpent, he may well have remembered the story. Possibly he wished that he, too, could make such a discovery.

If he did, he was not to be disappointed. At first, he thought that it was just a shadow on the water. But then he looked again, and presently he put his telescope to his eye.

'Ye gods!' he exclaimed. 'Come and see this.'

His officers and some of the sailors joined him. The

telescope was passed from hand to hand, and they were all amazed at what they saw.

Basking in the afternoon sunshine, taking it easy upon the surface of the ocean, was a most uncommon creature. Its head and neck were of truly enormous size, and there was the mass of mane that McQuhae had talked about.

'By heavens,' said one of the sailors, 'it's the Great Serpent its very self.'

'Never mind that,' said Captain Smith. 'Lower a boat. We're going to take a closer look at him.'

They used the longboat. The first officer took the tiller and the sailors bent their backs to the oars.

As he watched them, Captain Smith's surprise increased. By all that was reasonable, the monster should be taking at least some small interest in its visitors. If it was indeed the creature that Captain McQuhae had watched, it had, presumably, seen a sailing ship before.

And if this was the one at which the American brig had fired its assortment of hardware, it must have decided that these vessels were things to be avoided. Or was that expecting too much? By all accounts, the brontosaurus was an enormous creature and, in some respects, not unlike a sea monster in appearance. And yet, if these reports are correct, its brain was little bigger than a sparrow's.

Perhaps this Goliath of the deep was really a massive moron: an unintelligent colossus, a fearsome-looking fool, which could not put two and two together, and could not learn – even from experience.

Whatever it was, it simply lay there, heaving gently up and down in time with the waves, and paying not the smallest attention to the boatload of mariners which could (according to how you viewed these things) provide a tasty snack, or else be a deadly peril.

With eyes which could, in his opinion, scarcely be

trusted, Captain Smith watched one of the seamen making a rope fast around the monster's neck, and then saw the boat turn round for its return trip to the ship. And all the while, the idiot beast batted not so much as an eyelid, nor displayed the slightest signs of anger, greed, fear, amusement, interest, nor anything else which, if it were half the creature its size suggested, it should have been feeling.

Less than half an hour after the longboat's departure, the creature was being hauled on board. It was, indeed, one hundred feet long, and it was about four feet in diameter. There was the thick mass of mane, and there was the patch of white at the throat. It was exactly like the creature reports had suggested, except in one very fundamental particular.

For this was no mysterious monster. It was, simply, a colossal collection of seaweed. No wonder it had displayed so little interest. Disappointed that his name would not go down in history as the first man to capture a sea serpent, Captain Smith ordered the mass of marine vegetation to be thrown overboard.

'And make it lively, men,' he gruffly commanded. 'We've wasted enough time with this damn thing as it is.'

What, then, are we to make of these stories? The creature which dragged two men to their deaths, and caused the death of another, was obviously no harmless conglomeration of seaweed. But what about the others? For an inert mass of vegetation, Mr Maclean's inquisitive visitor sounds to have been reasonably active; and, before we dismiss it as a figment of the minister's imagination, we have to remember that there were several other witnesses – namely, the crews of the other thirteen boats.

This book is about sea mysteries, and so Loch Ness – which is a large lake – is out of bounds. But sea serpents and sea monsters appear to belong to a similar tribe to that of 'Nessie', and a man would have to be very foolish to state, categorically, that there is no such thing as a Loch Ness monster.

Perhaps, after a fashion, these creatures are like flying saucers. In a very large number of instances, they can be given a perfectly rational, rather dull, explanation. But, so long as there is one which cannot be accounted for, we have to admit the possibility that they exist.

The creature which attacked that sailing ship so long ago was obviously of a different species to the other apparitions. Its large tentacle suggested that it was an outsize member of the octopus family. On the other hand, these creatures usually live in the shelter of rocks, caves, and wrecks. They seldom, if ever, come to the surface, and they are lazy brutes. They will attack anything which comes too close to them, but they never set out on voyages in search of a snack.

It seems more likely that the aggressor in this case was a fabulous monster, which moves by jet propulsion, known as the giant squid. In fiction, one of Jules Verne's heroes had a battle with a member of the species, and there is evidence that they exist in real life.

Of the other sightings, all seem to have been in the shape of large serpents. The effect of horse's mane has been common to most of them; they have moved with an undulating motion, which has sometimes produced the effect of a series of humps; they have always appeared to be harmless, no matter how frightening they may have looked; and they have usually been seen in summer months.

Undoubtedly, as the story of the *Peking* shows, some of them can be written off as illusions created by a large amount of seaweed. Basking sharks, which often swim in pairs with one behind the other, have sometimes been mistaken for a monster, and so have porpoises. There is a creature known as the ribbon fish, which is twenty and, sometimes, thirty feet long; and there is a giant cuttle-fish, which is at least forty feet long.

One report alleged that a sea serpent had been witnessed in deadly combat with a whale. It makes a good story, until one learns that giant squids are anything up to fifty feet long and whales, whenever they get the opportunity, like to eat them. This account could equally well be explained by the fact that the whale was busy disposing of a squid, and that one of the latter's tentacles was wrapped around its back.

However, one must remember that there is far more ocean than there is land on this planet, and that some of it is very deep indeed. Nobody should imagine that man, clever as he may imagine himself to be, has discovered all the creatures which inhabit this dark and largely unexplored world.

There are certainly sea snakes, which are highly dangerous creatures (one of them is four times more deadly than the lethally venomous cobra that lives on land), but these unlikeable reptiles breathe air. If the sea serpent belonged to the same species, it would have to come up to the surface at fairly regular intervals to fill its lungs. In which case, there is a reasonable chance that it would have been seen.

Perhaps, indeed, it *has* been seen – though not for a good many years. The last report was made in 1905 by the crew of a yacht off the coast of Brazil. What has it been up to since?

Finally, for those who would like there still to be *some* mystery in the world, and for whom news of a sea serpent would be good news, enormous eggs belonging to an eel have been discovered in the Pacific. These are far, far bigger than any larva that has ever been seen before. They suggest that, somewhere in the depths, there lives an eel which is so much bigger than any other eel that it might well be mistaken for a sea serpent. When, if ever, this giant is sighted, we may at last know the truth about this still unsolved mystery of the ocean.

5

The Girl in the Boat

According to her owners, the SS *Forfarshire* was a very fine vessel. She was, they told prospective passengers, fast, reliable, and most luxurious. When she was delivered to them in 1834, they liked her so much that they immediately ordered a sister ship. The cost was £22,000, which was a lot of money in those days, but they considered it well spent.

If you could afford to travel cabin class, there is no doubt that the *Forfarshire* was an extremely comfortable vessel. The saloon had been decorated by a famous artist; the food was good, and there was an excellent stock of wines. The passengers all agreed that a day or two at sea was a much better way of travelling from Hull to Dundee, than by the alternative method, which was by stage coach.

But if you could not afford such sumptuous accommodation, you had to travel steerage. Nowadays this might be described as second class, and it was certainly a shabby alternative to first. The passengers were housed in a stuffy cabin right up front in the fo'c'sle. Every pitch and toss of the ship was a much bigger pitch and toss than the cabin-class travellers experienced in their state rooms amidships.

When conditions allowed it, she travelled at nine knots, which was reasonably fast. Her steam engines were as reliable as any of that period – and so were her boilers, though that is not saying a great deal. Because nobody had gained very much experience of them, marine boilers had a dangerous habit of exploding, and killing the men who fed them with coal. The *Forfarshire*'s never actually exploded, but they were by far the least technically attractive feature of the ship.

If you had believed the advertisements, you might have thought that she was a large ocean greyhound – a foretaste of the great Cunarders which, presently, were to conquer the North Atlantic. In fact, she was quite small – about half the size of a clipper ship, with a narrow hull which suddenly widened out in the middle to accommodate the paddle wheels. She had two masts with provisions for sails on them, a tall thin funnel, and an iron hull, which was something of a novelty. In those days, most ships were still built of wood.

Information about who travelled in her on her voyages up and down the North Sea is hard to discover. No passenger lists were ever compiled: indeed, it was rather like boarding a bus with an eccentric conductor in charge. There were no fixed fares. You struck a deal with the captain and, when you had agreed a sum satisfactory to both sides, you paid him.

When, on September 5th, 1838, the *Forfarshire* left the Humber for Dundee, her holds were crammed with boiler plates and textile machinery, clothing and hardware, and countless cakes of soap.

We know very little about her cabin-class passengers, except that there was an elderly couple and their nephew on board, and there may have been a party of Russians. On the other hand, this might have been a number of businessmen returning home from Russia from one of the Baltic ports via Hull.

There was definitely a clergyman on board, a baker, a weaver, a woman and her two children, and a talkative

Irishman who was extremely pessimistic by nature. These were all travelling steerage. All told, there were probably thirty-nine passengers, plus the master (Captain John Humble) and his wife, two mates, twelve seamen, two engineers, two firemen, two coal trimmers, and two stewards – making a total of sixty-three.

It was a blustery evening when, at half past six, they let go the ropes and, to the tune of plonk-plonk-plonk from the paddle wheels, edged out into the Humber. The weaver, who was on his way home, stood at the rail and looked across the river. Nearby, two more paddlers – the *Pegasus* and the *Inisfail*, both of them bound for Leith – were also taking advantage of the ebb tide to help them down to the North Sea.

Standing beside the weaver was the Irishman named Donovan. The latter turned to the little man from Dundee, and said: 'I don't like it.'

The weaver, without taking his eye from the *Pegasus* and *Inisfail*, asked: 'What don't you like?'

'The boilers. I fear the very worst.'

'Why? Are you an engineer, or something?'

'No,' said Donovan, 'but I believe what I see. Before we cast off, they were inspecting those boilers. Now – I ask you. They aren't going to do that just for fun, are they? They *know* something, don't they?'

'And what,' asked the weaver, 'are they supposed to know?'

'That they may burst. That they may send this whole living kingdom into heaven by some great explosion. All they're asking themselves is: "Will it happen *this* trip?"'

It occurred to the weaver that if his companion had such misgivings, he might have done better to have stayed on shore. However, he said nothing. On most ships there is a passenger who talks too much and irritates the others with his chatter. Donovan, the weaver decided, was just such a case, and he had no intention of becoming the first victim.

By nine o'clock, the *Forfarshire* had reached the open sea. A strong wind was blowing, and the motion of the paddler was extremely uncomfortable. A number of the passengers had already prudently taken to their bunks. Others had remained on deck, firm in their belief that the best cure for seasickness is to feel the wind on your face.

Butting into the teeth of the storm, the small steamer plodded northwards, her speed cut back to six knots. Down in the steerage-class cabin, conditions were awful. Many of the passengers were feeling (and being) very ill indeed, and the ventilation system did little to freshen the place up. At four o'clock in the morning, the weaver gave up all further attempts to sleep and went on deck. He found Donovan leaning over the rail, looking unhappily towards the west.

'A sailor just told me there's Flamborough Head over there. Wish I were on it,' the Irishman said.

'It's not very comfortable, is it,' the weaver admitted. It was something of an understatement. The ship was producing a horrible corkscrew motion, half pitch and half roll, which brought out the worst features of both. Her girders were groaning in the way that girders do in a rough sea – as if the very heart of the vessel is protesting at such treatment – and the wind was shrieking its hatred through the rigging.

'They've got both the deck pumps working,' Donovan muttered, 'and, from what I hear, there's trouble with the boilers. I said there would be, didn't I?'

'Don't tell me they've exploded,' the weaver said.

'No – not that. You'd be up on a cloud playing a harp, if they had. But there's other things that can happen. If they don't make enough steam, what's to drive the engines? And if the engines go out of action, what's to become of us?'

'She has sails, surely,' the weaver pointed out.

'Huh!' Donovan grunted, disgusted at his friend's optimism.

As it happened, the starboard boiler *was* giving trouble. It had sprung a leak. It was not, as the chief engineer took pains to tell the captain, serious. It could no doubt be repaired.

As the day wore on, the wind veered and the *Forfarshire* made better speed in spite of her leaking boiler. But the weather was becoming even worse. The dark sky, a mass of torn grey shreds of cloud tumbling in agony from one horizon to the other: this, and the vile motion of the ship, which seemed to be locked in combat with the sea, did little to cheer anyone up.

In the first-class saloon, those who felt strong enough ate well and drank well, and said: 'Even in this weather, she's better than that frightful stage coach.' In steerage, they simply suffered.

Donovan was enclosed in his own nightmare about impending doom. Unfortunately for everyone else, vestiges of the bad dream kept on leaking out, 'She'll never survive this,' he'd confide. Or: 'I hear the starboard boiler's getting worse.' Or: 'Note how none of us has seen the captain today. He has no time to talk with the passengers. He has one huge worry on his mind.'

In fact, they did see the captain that day. At eight o'clock in the evening – two hours after they had passed the Farne Islands off the coast of Northumberland – he came round with a steward to collect the fares.

He parried questions from the passengers with such enigmatic sounds as 'Ah!' and 'Eh?' and 'Hum . . .', and he pretended not to hear, when Donovan remarked that it was 'cheaper to have a posh funeral from an undertaker than to travel in this floating coffin'.

As the night wore on, the wind backed to the north and increased to gale force. Sometimes it seemed as if the world was going to end, but this did not deter the cabin-class travellers. They undressed and went to bed. Down in steerage people huddled unhappily in their bunks and waited for the next outrage that fate might have in store for them.

By midnight, they were off Berwick-on-Tweed. The gale was blowing as lustily as ever and, to make matters worse, the visibility had dropped almost to nothing. Captain Humble was standing by the wheel when a dim shape came stumbling down the deck towards him. It was the chief engineer.

'Can I speak to you for a moment, Captain?' he yelled against the noise of the storm. Captain Humble ushered him into the chart room. 'We can talk better here,' he said.

'I'm afraid there's trouble,' the engineer said. 'The boilers are sick again. I can't make enough steam for the engines.'

'There's nothing you can do? No repairs you can carry out?'

'None. This is a job for a shipyard. It might even be we'll have to get new ones.'

'We'll have to use the sails, then,' the captain said. 'But we can't make any progress against this lot. We're punching the wind and the tide at present. I'll have to turn about and put into North Shields.'

The engineer went below to examine, for the umpteenth time, his leaking boilers. The captain went back on deck. It was now raining very heavily indeed.

He went up to the first mate, and told him of the trouble down in the engine room. 'I want sails set to keep her off the land,' he said. 'And I'm going to turn about. We'll head for North Shields, but that's for later. Until this gale has blown itself out, we'll shelter in the lee of the Farne Islands.'

'Yes, Captain.'

The weaver had once again given up hopes of sleep, and had decided that, even with a gale blowing, life on deck would be better than the cramped and sickly confines of the steerage accommodation. He had been clinging to the mainmast rigging when the captain was giving his orders to the mate. The words 'Farne Islands' were blown across to him on the wind, and he remembered having seen them on a map.

There were about twenty-five of them, he recalled The nearest to land was some two miles offshore – the farthest, five miles. It would, he imagined, be difficult to grope a passage safely into their midst with such poor visibility and this terrible gale blowing. But that, he told himself, was the captain's problem. He imagined that such an able man found no difficulty in dealing with such things.

For the time being, he had worries enough of his own. He was now thoroughly drenched, and the wind was cutting through his sodden clothes. It might be bad down below in the fo'c'sle, but nothing, surely, could be worse than this. He decided to make for shelter.

Going forward along the wildly pitching deck was like travelling over a helter-skelter. One moment, you seemed to be climbing a mountain, the next you were trying to stop yourself tumbling into a valley. By holding on to one fixture and then another, he eventually made it, though he nearly fell down the ladder on the last bit.

Donovan, needless to say, was awake.

'The engines are out of action, eh?' It was more of a statement than a question.

'I believe so,' the weaver said. 'How did you know?'

'You can tell. Isn't there a kind of silence about the ship? And you can't hear the thump of the paddle wheels in the water. It's as if this stinking tub is half dead already.'

The weaver wondered how such things could be noticed against the yelling of the gale and the groaning of the ship, but he did not say so.

'I think I'll put on some dry clothes,' he said. 'I'm soaked right through.'

'Dry clothes is right,' Donovan said. 'You'll need them when the time comes.'

While he was changing, it occurred to the weaver that he ought to put Donovan's mind at rest about one or two things. 'Listen,' he said, 'you worry too much. Captain Humble is a very experienced man. Things like this are happening all the time to professional seamen. He doesn't have to think twice about what to do.'

'So he doesn't,' Donovan said. 'I hope you're right, but will you tell me how he's going to get us out of this big mess?'

'I heard him tell the mate that we're putting about and running for the shelter of the Farne Islands.'

Donovan, who had never heard of this litter of rocks and tiny morsels of land, was silent for a moment or two.

Then he said: 'Farne Islands – if you ask me, there's no such place. He was making it up. Here we are in the middle of the ocean, with no engines working, and he imagines islands. Sailors sometimes go mad, you know – and that, my friend, is what is happening to Captain

Humble. God rest the poor devil's soul when the time comes.'

Unfortunately for Captain Humble, the Farne Islands were only too real. There were two lighthouses on them. One was on the Inner Farne, which is relatively close to the shore; and one was on Longstone, which is the most seaward of the group. Humble's intention was to keep the Inner Farne light on his port side. Once he had passed it, the sea ought to be calmer and he would be able to drop anchor.

Both mates were on deck by now. 'Keep your eyes well open,' he told them. 'We should see the light quite soon'.

The time was five minutes to four in the morning.

Rain was still battering away at the deck, and the visibility was not improving. Presently, the second mate called: 'There's your light, Captain – but something's wrong. It's away there over to starboard.'

'Yes, I see,' the captain said.

At this moment, there came a startled cry from the look-out. 'Breakers ahead,' the man yelled. The tide, which was now running hard south, was driving the *Forfarshire* towards an area of seething white water.

'Hard to port,' Humble barked. The helmsman spun the wheel round for all he was worth, but the ship did not answer. The inert paddle wheels made her very hard to manoeuvre, and the tide was a relentless demon. One might have imagined that the sea had literally picked up the ship and thrown her at the water ahead.

Seconds passed and then, with a great jolt, the *Forfarshire* hit the rock.

'Get everyone on deck,' the captain ordered, 'and make ready the boats. Quickly now – I don't know how long she'll last.'

Waves were breaking right over the vessel, scattering their foam in her rigging and walloping their water down on to the deck. With an unholy din, the hull withdrew from the rock for a moment, and then plunged back on it. This happened again and again, with the fearful com-

'Waves were breaking right over the vessel . . . walloping their water down on to the deck'

plaint of metal scraping against the rough surface; a pause, and a forward thrust, and a sound like an explosion, as the bottom was slammed down on the ledge half hidden by the restless sea.

The starboard boat had been swung outwards the moment she struck. But that was about as far as order prevailed. Figures from the cabin-class accommodation, wearing only their night attire, struggled to get near it. One young man, who was holding his trousers up in front of his nightshirt, actually made it. His elderly aunt and uncle did not.

Without waiting for instructions, the boat was lowered over the side. It crashed down into the sea below, seemed about to turn over, and then steadied itself.

'For heaven's sake, Mr Duncan,' Captain Humble said to his first mate, 'get down there and take charge.'

Without replying, the mate jumped. He missed the boat by about a foot, struggled towards it, and was hauled on board. And that, for the time being, was the last anyone saw of it. The current swept it away. Within seconds, it was lost in the darkness.

All the other lifeboats had been destroyed by the heavy seas which were still crashing across the decks

Fifteen minutes after she had hit the rock, the *Forfarshire* broke in half. The entire section aft of the paddle wheels was swept away. With it went Captain Humble, his other officer, many of the crew and most of the cabin-class passengers.

Up on the fo'c'sle head, the steerage travellers clustered in a small, frightened, group.

'I told you this would happen,' Donovan said to the weaver.

'Oh – shut up!' that normally patient man said. He had had just about enough.

Gradually the sky became lighter, and they found that they were perched precariously on a large rock which, they afterwards discovered, was known as Big Harcker. A string of islands stretched away to the west, and it became horribly obvious that Captain Humble had just made his first and last mistake. The light which the second mate had reported had not been the Inner Farne at all. It was the Longstone, and it had to be from that lighthouse that help, if any, would come.

The weaver was considering the situation, when he became aware of a quiet voice calling them to order. 'My name's Tulloch,' the voice said. 'I'm the ship's carpenter, and I'd better take charge. Let's see who we have here.'

There were twelve of them in all. Among them were the ship's cook, a woman with her two children, the baker, the clergyman, and Mr Donovan whose powers of survival seemed to be almost as great as his pessimism.

The clergyman was seeking what little cover he could in the shelter of the engine housing, but it was not enough. Just after dawn, the poor man died from exposure. Later, the two children also died.

'What do you think of our hopes, Mr Tulloch?' the weaver asked.

'Not too bad, not too good,' the carpenter said. He was large and capable, and calm. 'The nearest boats are at Sunderland, and it will take them some time to get here – even if they managed to put out in this sea.'

'But what about the lighthouse?'

'I couldn't say how they're placed. I reckon it would take three strong men to reach us from there. It wouldn't be at all easy with these strong currents, and they might easily capsize. I really don't think I'd count on the lighthouse.'

And so they waited, and shivered, and were afraid.

It was Tulloch who first saw it: the merest speck of a boat struggling across the water from Longstone. 'I don't like to hope for too much,' he said, 'but here's hope. The lighthouse keeper and his mate are trying to reach us.'

They waited and they watched, and the boat, guided by perfect seamanship, came nearer and nearer. There were, indeed, two figures on board. One of them was tall, the other was short and slender – too small, it seemed, to handle the oars under such conditions as these. But the oars swung rhythmically backwards and forwards, dipping faultlessly into the water and thrusting the little boat forward.

Presently, after an agony of time, it came alongside the wreck. One of the oarsmen stood up. He was a man in his middle years, tall, upright and with a stern face which looked as if it seldom smiled.

'Make her fast, Grace,' he said, 'and we'll see what's to be done.'

The weaver looked down. The other member of the crew, who was about twenty-three years old, was a girl. Somehow, by what miracle he never knew, an ageing man and a frail young woman had brought a rowing boat across a wild expanse of water on a voyage which, in the opinion of so able and experienced a man as the ship's carpenter, required the combined powers of three strong men.

But then he busied himself in helping Tulloch organize the retreat from the rock. The weaver had many things to think about, but the most important was that, for the first time in several hours, he knew that he was going to remain alive.

William Darling, the keeper of the Longstone lighthouse, looked exactly what he was: a strict, deeply religious man, who regarded playing-cards as 'the Devil's books' and permitted no light literature in his home. He and Mrs Darling had nine children of whom, at the time of the *Forfarshire* wreck, only Grace was with them. She was a delicate young woman, but she knew how to handle a boat and she had been out with her father several times in the twenty-one-foot long craft that belonged to the lighthouse.

It was she who had sighted the wreck and called her father. When he first studied it through his telescope, he could see no survivors. This was no doubt because Tulloch had found a sheltered spot for them in the lee of the rock.

Just before seven o'clock (three hours after the *Forfarshire* had struck), however, he noted some movement.

'Somebody has to get over there, Grace,' he said. 'I doubt if the boats from Sunderland will reach them in time. It has to be you and I.'

'Yes, Father,' she said.

Mrs Darling helped them to launch the boat. It was one and three-quarters of a mile from the lighthouse to the wreck. Fortunately, it was in sheltered water for most of the way, but the going was none the less hard, and there were several difficult patches of water.

It needed two trips to get everybody safely over to the lighthouse. On the first, they returned with four men and the woman. Two of the men then went back with Darling to bring the others to safety.

Some while later, the ship's boat, which had managed to survive its turbulent passage away from the wreck (how she ever managed to escape having her bottom ripped out on one of the rocks is another miracle), was picked up by a sloop outward bound from Montrose. There were nine survivors aboard her, including the young man who deserted his aunt and uncle and clung so tenaciously to his trousers. It turned out afterwards that the pockets were crammed with gold coins, which probably explains everything. They were landed safely at Tynemouth, and the adventure and the tragedy of the SS *Forfarshire* were over.

Of the sixty-three people on board her, forty-three had died. Had it not been for the indomitable will of the lighthouse keeper's daughter, eleven more would have perished.

As for Grace Darling, rewards and honours were showered upon her. Her portrait was painted seven times in twelve days; the owner of a circus offered her a contract to make personal appearances; and there were so many requests for locks of her hair that her parents began to fear she might go bald. But all this fame never changed her. Perhaps she, more than anyone else, was aware of the mystery which took place early that September morning: the mystery of how one man and one small, delicate young woman, could do the work of three strong sailors. That is the mystery of Grace Darling and the *Forfarshire*, and nobody has been able to explain it.

6

Pity the Poor Dutchman

Within the sea's collection of mysteries, there are a few tantalizing cases which have never been solved, and for which not even the *vestige* of a solution has been found. As studies in the astonishing, they are immense. As stories, however, they are very short – simply because so little is known about them.

Take, for example, the case of the sailing ship *Ellen Austin*. She was scudding across the Atlantic one day in 1881. The wind was fair; all her sails were set; and the sunshine was flashing amiable messages off the tops of the waves.

Presently, she drew level with a schooner which was on a parallel course. She, too, was under full sail, and she was making very good speed. But, surprisingly, there was no one on deck.

The *Ellen Austin*'s master hailed her. When he received no reply, he turned to one of his officers and said: 'Reckon there's something wrong with that vessel. We'd better take a closer look.'

Led by the mate, a small party of sailors set off in one of the ship's boats and boarded the apparently unmanned schooner. For the next hour or so, the two vessels sailed together.

By now it was mid-afternoon, and the sky ahead was black. Before very long, a thick sponge of cloud wiped the sun off the face of the sky. The wind got up and heavy rain fell. The *Ellen Austin*'s crew could no longer see the schooner. And, in any case, they were too busy taking in sail and coping with the sudden challenge of the storm.

An hour or two later, the rain stopped and the wind calmed down. The sun came back again, and the murk of the squall sped away behind them to the east. The schooner was still there, but she appeared to be handling badly.

At first, the *Ellen Austin*'s captain assumed that something had been damaged by the squall. But when he picked up his telescope and studied her carefully, he saw that, once again, there was nobody on deck.

'Get a boat ready,' he said. 'I'm going over to see what's happened.'

He remained there long enough to discover that the storm had done no damage, and that there was not a soul on board her. Of the vessel's original crew, there was no sign, and his own men had vanished too.

Back on his own ship, he called for volunteers to form a further prize crew. Nobody came forward.

'You're all of you making a mistake,' he said. 'That's a fine ship over there, and the salvage money will be considerable. Now – listen carefully. This is what I propose . . .'

The plan he outlined amounted to a promise that anyone who dared the mystery of the strange schooner would be very generously rewarded. For a few moments, there was silence. Then three or four men stepped forward. 'We'll have a go,' they said.

A few minutes later, the new crew rowed over to the schooner and went aboard her. One man took over the helm, checked his course, and the vessel sprang eagerly forward as the wind filled her sails. Of the two ships, she was the faster, and so the captain of the *Ellen Austin* was not particularly surprised when he watched her draw steadily ahead and presently vanish over the horizon.

The final surprise was to come later. For, after she had disappeared in the direction of the nearest American port, that uncanny schooner was never seen again. And nor were any of the men who had sailed in her.

What can one make of that? A thriller writer would doubtless have a fine time building up intricate patterns of theories; but that would be a work of the imagination. Factually, there is nothing more to tell. That the schooner was lost at sea, there can be no doubt. Conceivably her original crew abandoned ship unnecessarily – in much the way that the ship's company of the *Mary Celeste* probably did. But what about the party from the *Ellen Austin*? Did they abandon ship as well? Unnecessarily? That, surely, is too much of a coincidence.

Consider another example. In the year 1821, two brigs were on a voyage exploring the coasts of Arabia, Madagascar, and East Africa. One of the vessels was named *Barracouta*; and it is important to remember that there were a number of unorthodox features about her rigging, which made her quite unmistakable. 'You could spot the old *Barracouta* anywhere,' they used to say.

The other ship's name was *Severn*. She was commanded by a captain in the Royal Navy named Owen.

There they were, then – these two brigs on similar assignments which were to take them over thousands of miles of ocean. Late one afternoon, *Severn* was cruising down the coast of South West Africa towards Simon's Bay, where she was due to anchor in the morning. Captain Owen had been busy in his cabin, writing up the log. When he came on deck, he noticed another brig about two miles away to leeward.

'That's funny,' he said to the mate, 'she looks like the *Barracouta*.'

'I'm sure she is the *Barracouta*,' the mate replied.

'Yes – yes. I think you're right. But she has no business to be in this area,' the captain said. 'Still – there's no mistaking her rigging. There's not another brig like her'.

The two vessels maintained their courses, and Captain Owen thought no more about it. Just as the sun was setting, however, *Barracouta* hove to and lowered a boat.

'What do you make of that?' Captain Owen asked the mate, who was studying the incident through his telescope.

'Looks like somebody's fallen overboard, sir,' he said. 'They're picking him up.'

'Careless idiot,' the captain said.

Barracouta got under way again, just as night was falling. During the hours of darkness, she did not display any navigation lights, and there were no glimmers through her portholes. Beyond telling the look-out to be sure there was no danger of a collision, Captain Owen made no comment about it. He was, after all, sailing down an unknown coast, with no charts to guide him, and he had plenty of other things to think about.

The following morning dawned bright. The clear water of Simon's Bay rippled in blue and gold beneath the warm sun, and there was the green promise of land a mile or two ahead. Presently, the *Severn* dropped anchor, and Captain Owen went below for his breakfast.

'I imagine the *Barracouta* will be here soon,' he told the officer of the watch. 'Let me know when she arrives.'

But the *Barracouta* did not arrive that day, nor on any other day. She was busy some distance to the north. As Captain Owen was to learn later, at the time when he (what does one say? 'Saw'? 'Thought he saw?' 'Was certain he'd seen?') the brig, she had, in fact, been 300 miles away.

Very well then – it wasn't the *Barracouta* that he and the other members of the *Severn*'s crew had seen. It was some other vessel of the same class.

It is a beautiful explanation – absolutely watertight, except for one thing. No other vessel of the *Barracouta*'s class *ever* visited that particular corner of the Indian Ocean.

And then there are some mysteries to which the explanation is even more improbable than the event itself. Such is the case of the *Flying Dutchman*. During the past 300 years, sailors have claimed to have seen this strange vessel, lit by a weird light, with her demented captain and her monstrous cabin boy, sailing the ocean for ever, and bringing bad luck to all who see her. Yes – there are sailors who say they've seen her, but they'd have the devil of a job to prove it.

The tale of the *Flying Dutchman* is really a fable which doesn't come off. It is one of those stories with a hidden moral: the sort of thing our ancestors believed improved the minds of the young. In a way, it was a literary confidence trick. The author led you right up the garden path, before revealing that, all the time, he'd really been preaching a sermon.

The *Flying Dutchman* story was first set down on paper by a Frenchman. Doubtless his intentions were very high-minded; but it is hard to imagine what, exactly, he hoped to achieve in the mind-improving line. Anyway, let us take a look at it.

As the central character (who is obviously cast as the villain) we have a Dutch sea captain; a stubborn old rascal who didn't like being pushed around. We see him, somehow, as a perky, red-faced individual, with a mouth which could smile easily enough when things warranted it, but could equally well harden up into a firm, obstinate line. He was a man who enjoyed life. He liked to smoke his pipe, and he was very partial to beer. Furthermore, he was one of those rare beings who do not know the meaning of fear.

The tempest might rage, and the wild seas might batter his ship, but this sort of thing did not bother him in the slightest. He just puffed away at his pipe, took another swig of ale, and continued on his course.

One day, this intrepid seaman was on a voyage to the Cape of Good Hope. Shortly after his ship had left the good-natured Trade Winds, they encountered a strong head wind. Our Dutch friend was not the slightest bit daunted. He kept a full head of sail set; sat on top of the quarterdeck skylight, and filled his pipe with tobacco.

The wind increased to gale force, until it seemed as if it must tear the masts out of the hull. The sky was black. There were vivid shafts of lightning stabbing the sea, and the waves were like the sides of large black buildings towering over the ship.

'Bring me another beer,' the skipper told the cabin boy, when his pipe was drawing nicely.

The crew and the passengers became very worried indeed. 'For heaven's sake – can't you bring him to his senses,' one of the latter said to the mate. 'We'll have to turn back. Surely you can make him see that.'

The mate nervously approached him. 'Begging your pardon, sir,' he said, 'but the passengers are nervous. Mightn't it be a good idea to put about?'

Captain van Whatever-his-name-was blew out a slow,

luxurious plume of tobacco smoke, took a deep drink from his mug, and said: 'Rubbish'.

The mate implored him. The second mate implored him. A delegation of passengers implored him. But he simply told them they were all talking nonsense.

In fact, they were not. Before very long, there was a terrible rending of wood and tearing of canvas, and the topmasts were blown away. And the captain remained seated on the skylight, sipping his ale and smoking like a tramp steamer's funnel. And laughing – laughing as if the whole thing were a ridiculous charade that only a fool could take seriously.

Possibly his sailors *were* fools, but one could hardly blame them. At all events, a party of them presently came up on to the poop and approached the smirking, beer-swigging skipper.

'You can call it what you like,' the ringleader said. 'You can say it's mutiny, if you will, but I and the others insist that you make for shelter. Unless you do this, we'll take over the ship.'

The captain said nothing. He carefully put down his pipe and his mug, eased himself off the skylight, and walked towards the ringleader. With a quick movement, he caught the wretched man off balance, picked him up and slung him over the side.

'Anyone else want a swim?' he asked, resuming his seat and re-lighting his pipe.

Up to this point, the story is straightforward enough. It might all have happened. The captain would have been eccentric – even a little bit mad – but it is all perfectly plausible. He might have honestly believed that his ship could withstand such a gale without being damaged. Perhaps, when the masts were ripped away, nobody was more surprised than he was. In any case, no captain worthy of the rank likes to receive instructions from his passengers, and certainly not from his crew.

And did all that beer go to his head? Was he a little drunk at the time? This appears to be doubtful, for ale was the very stuff of life to him, and it would have taken more than a few mugs of Dutch lager to make old van Thing light-headed.

But now we move dramatically, if totally unconvincingly, into the realm of the supernatural. It is rather like the sort of situation you would find in a cinema if, through some mistake, the projectionist inserted a reel from a Bible epic into the midst of a Western.

There was the gale howling, and the sea smashing, and the rigging rending, the sails being ripped from the spars, and the people all halfway out of their minds with fear, and Captain van Stubborn sitting calmly through it all, sipping and smoking and finding it all rather a giggle.

And then, suddenly, the heavens opened and a Form (that, at any rate is what the French writer called it) alighted on the quarterdeck. It may have been an angel: it could have been a devil. It came from the way-out-yonder and made everybody even more afraid, except the captain. Poor old van – there he sat, still full of self-confidence and not even bothering to doff his cap to the apparition.

'Who wants a peaceful passage?' he observed – apropos of nothing in particular. 'I don't.' And he took a pistol which he carried in his belt and fired a shot at the Form.

That, perhaps, is the first lesson that every aspiring marksman should learn: never take a pot shot at a Supernatural Form. You are bound to lose. In this case, the bullet simply bounced off Itself, came back on a return trip and went slap through the captain's own hand. Not unnaturally, he was very angry.

If you *must* box, for goodness sake make sure that your opponent is a perfectly ordinary mortal. The captain, in his rage, tried to lash out at the Thing, but it was quite useless. His arm simply fell limply to his side as if it were paralysed.

'Now,' said the Form, 'we'll play it *my* way.'

And really, when one comes to think of it, it was a pretty rotten way. The captain was condemned to:

(*a*) Sail round and round the world for ever, with no rest and never reaching an anchorage.

(*b*) Be denied all supplies of beer and tobacco.

(*c*) Have only gall (horrible stuff – it's too complicated to explain here) to drink and red-hot iron to eat.

(*d*) Everybody was to leave the ship except the cabin boy, who would be the captain's companion on his eternal voyage. But, poor lad, he was to undergo a considerable transformation. Horns were to grow out of his head; he was to have the muzzle of a tiger and a skin rougher than that of a dogfish. Goodness only knows what the innocent young fellow had done to deserve it, but that was what the Form said.

(*e*) The captain was to have no sleep at any time. If he nodded off for so much as a second, a sword would pierce his body.

(*f*) Because (according to the Form) he liked to torment sailors, he would become the evil spirit of the seas. In other words, his ship would bring misfortune to anyone who set eyes upon it.

And that was that. With a WOOM-PH! the Form was

'. . . he was to have the muzzle of a tiger and a skin rougher than that of a dog-fish'

gone, and so were all the passengers and the crew except the by now hideously transformed cabin boy.

It makes a good enough story, but one cannot help feeling sorry for poor old Captain van Why-didn't-*any-body*-bother-to-write-his-name-down? He was just a simple sailor who, as we remarked earlier, didn't like being pushed around.

Rapid Footnote to Readers: if you insist on a rational explanation of the *Flying Dutchman* sightings, you are referred to the small print in the Form's list. Among the items appeared one which said that the ship could change her appearance at will. It meant that she could look like *any* vessel. Add to this the natural phenomenon of St Elmo's fire, which says a dictionary, is 'A luminous electrical discharge sometimes seen on ships during storms', and you get the effect.

7

The Sunken Gold

It was May 19th, 1922. England had been enjoying a few days of mild summer weather. There had been a rush of early holidaymakers to the beaches whilst, at Tilbury, the P & O liner, *Egypt,* was preparing for a voyage to India.

She was a steamship of 8,000 tons, with a black hull, two black funnels, and a superstructure which was painted in that certain shade of buff which made all P & O boats immediately recognizable.

When the *Egypt* was launched in 1897, she and her sister ship, the *India*, had been the two largest liners in the P & O fleet. Now she was twenty-five years old, and there were many larger vessels on the route to the Far East. But she still plodded backwards and forwards at a steady speed of fifteen knots and could carry 500 passengers in a good deal of comfort. Although she was elderly, there were no immediate plans to retire her.

In those days there were no air services to the Far East and you had to make the journey by sea. Some travelled the entire distance by this method. Others, to save time, went overland to Marseilles. The shipping company ran a special train from Victoria Station in London. It linked up with a cross-Channel steamer from Dover to Calais, and then with an express, which sped down the length of France and arrived at Marseilles in time to meet the liner.

On the day when this story begins, 40 passengers went aboard the *Egypt* at Tilbury. In her crew there were 86 European officers and men, 208 Asian sailors, stewards and firemen.

But the interesting feature of this particular trip was the liner's cargo. Apart from the more commonplace items (which included a £2,000 shipment of sugar), she was carrying the largest load of bullion to be dispatched to India since the days before the First World War. There was £674,000's worth of gold bars, £165,000's worth of gold coins, and £215,000's worth of silver bars – all of which added up to £1,054,000's worth of the most valuable freight in the world.

In the late afternoon, a bevy of tugs, fussing importantly round the liner, helped her away from her berth and out into the Thames estuary. The plume of foam at her bow thickened; the vessel seemed to shake herself as the engineers built up her speed; gongs sounded throughout the passenger accommodation, calling people to the first sitting of dinner. The routine for the voyage was already established. The travellers were settling down for what seemed likely to be a thoroughly pleasant trip.

On the following day, about twenty-two hours after the *Egypt* had left her berth at Tilbury, the French cargo steamer, *Seine*, slipped quietly away from the quayside at Brest. To look at, the *Seine* was no different from most other tramp steamers: a little bit shabby as became her hardworking occupation, with patches of rust on her hull and the colours on her funnel in need of touching up.

But the *Seine* was an unusual ship. Most of her voyages took her to ports in northern waters, where ice is an ever present peril. Consequently, her bow had been specially reinforced. She may have looked harmless enough, but she was a very tough vessel indeed. If, by any mischance, she were to ram an ordinary ship, there was no doubt about which of the two would survive the encounter.

As he worked his vessel down river towards the Atlantic, the *Seine*'s captain was not in the best of tempers. His radio transmitter had been out of action for about a year. He was continually making plans to have it put right, but there never seemed to be time. As the owners pointed out, a ship in port did not earn them any money. It was only when she was carrying cargo on the high seas that she was profitable. The repairs to the transmitter would have to wait. For the moment, there was a great deal of work to be done.

If, as you might say, the voice of the ship was silent, her eyes were soon to be blinded. There was a nasty, damp chill in the air, and the captain knew only too well what it meant. Out at sea, fog was building up. In those days, there was no such thing as radar, and everything depended on the alertness of human vision. With no devices to penetrate it, fog was probably the greatest peril of them all.

At the mouth of the river, the *Seine* dropped her pilot.

'A pleasant voyage captain,' he said as he left the bridge.

'I hope so.'

'This fog doesn't look too good.'

'It's bad.'

'Good luck, then.'

'Goodbye.'

The pilot climbed down the rope ladder to the small motor-boat, which was to take him across the short expanse of sea to the cutter. The *Seine*'s captain lit another cigarette, and rang down 'Half-speed ahead' on the engine-room telegraph.

'Blast this fog,' he muttered. Outside the wheelhouse, the first officer reached for the lanyard which operated the siren. With a wheezy groan, which suggested that she was suffering from laryngitis, the *Seine* announced her presence to any other vessels which were in the vicinity.

'It's becoming thicker than ever,' the first officer said.

The sea had been calm. Beneath hazy sunshine, the *Egypt* steamed south-westwards. At about 7 PM, they would be twenty miles off Ushant, the French headland which is one of the gateposts to the English Channel.

At half past six, most of the passengers went to their cabins to change for dinner. Captain Collyer, the liner's master, was working in his day room, when he received a call from the bridge.

Stepping out on deck, he noticed at once that the sunshine had gone. The liner was wrapped in a grey secret world of fog. He almost ran up the ladder to the bridge. Peering over the top of the rail, he could only just make out the foremast.

He turned to the fourth officer, who was stationed at the telegraph. 'Slow ahead,' he said. And then: 'Double all the look-outs'. The liner crept forward, moving through an uncanny silence which was broken only by the wail of her whistle, groping blind, baffled by the thick veil of mist which hung down through the dead air.

Something like 30,000 ships a year travelled through these waters, and the ears of everybody on deck were stretched to catch the sound of just one of them: an unseen menace, which might come quietly out of the fog to hazard the *Egypt*'s life.

At seven o'clock, they heard it: a faint groan coming from somewhere just forward of the port beam. 'Stop Engines,' Captain Collyer said. The bells of the telegraph were overwhelmed by the lusty rasp of her siren.

Two minutes later, they heard the other whistle again. This time, it was much nearer. And then, out of the fog, a patch of darkness suddenly assumed shape.

'Hard a' port,' Captain Collyer called to the quartermaster.

But it was too late. With a fearful jolt, the tough, strengthened bows of the *Seine* smashed into the side of the *Egypt*, crashing into number three hold and shattering the bulkhead which divided it from the boiler room.

Everything seemed to happen at once. The *Seine*,

'With a fearful jolt the bows of the Seine *smashed into the side of the* Egypt*'*

which had been virtually undamaged by the collision, backed away from the *Egypt*, and vanished as secretly as she had come.

Down in the boiler room, there was panic. The water was rushing in, and nothing could be done to close the watertight doors. The Lascar firemen were stampeding into the engine-room, pushing, shoving, climbing over one another – anything to get away from the death trap.

Up on deck, the alarm signals were sounding. Passengers were running on to the boat deck. Some were wearing their lifebelts. A number were not. The liner began to list and, as every second passed, it became more pronounced. Before very long, she was leaning over at an angle of thirty degrees.

In the radio room, the wireless operator was transmitting an S O S. The Royal Mail Steam Packet Company's liner, *Andes*, acknowledged the signal, so did the lighthouse on Ushant, and so did another ship. But, from the *Seine*, which was only a matter of yards away, there was silence.

Normally Indian crews were not given to panic. They had a thoroughly good record in both world wars, and the behaviour of the Lascars in the *Egypt* was entirely untypical. The trouble was probably started by the terrified stokers from the boiler room, who had been scared out of their wits. It set off a wave of terror, which resulted in a number of them trying to rush the lifeboats. They got away with numbers one and two boats, before the ship's officers regained a certain amount of control.

The inhabitants of the *Egypt* took to the water in their various ways. Some escaped by lifeboat. In one of them an Army officer had drawn his revolver and was threatening to shoot the Indians and Goanese who seemed to be hazarding the craft's safety. He fired two shots. Afterwards he stated that he had pointed his gun into the air. He had not meant to hurt anybody. It was just a warning.

In fact, he hit a seaman and a fireman, who were clambering down the ropes.

On one boat, the running gear was faulty. Instead of making a controlled descent, it fell down towards the sea, smashed into the ship's side, and killed everyone on board.

A number of people jumped overboard, trusting to their lifejackets, and the possibility that somebody would pick them up.

And some stayed behind. The ship's doctor offered his place in one of the lifeboats to a lady passenger. Another woman came on deck without her lifejacket. The ship's printer, an elderly man from Dover who could not swim, said: 'Take mine, ma'am'. He remained on board. And so did a nun who refused the place that was offered her in one of the boats. She knelt down on deck and prayed. She was still on her knees when, twenty minutes after the *Seine* had struck, the *Egypt* buried her bows in the sea and sank head first into sixty-five fathoms of water.

Presently, the *Seine* reappeared, and the survivors were helped on board her. She turned round; crept back to the place whence she had come, and put them ashore at Brest.

A fortune sank with the *Egypt*. But gold, unlike human lives, can be recovered. Eventually most of the bullion was retrieved by an Italian salvage team. But it was a poor recompense for the fifteen passengers (seven of them women) and the seventy-one officers and men who went to their deaths in the eerie darkness of that foggy evening off Ushant.

You may now be asking where's the mystery? This, surely, is the straightforward story of a shipwreck? Sinister –

perhaps. Tragic – most certainly, But, surely, it can all be explained.

Yes – and then, again, no. There are all kinds of sea mysteries, and perhaps the most common are those in which ships, or people, or both, disappear and are never seen again. But there is also what you might call the Mystery of Coincidence, and the story of the *Egypt* is a sombre example of this type. It was strange, you must admit, that, of all the vessels which sailed past Ushant on that May evening in 1922, the only one which came to grief was carrying a record cargo of gold. It was strange, too, that with so much sea around her, the *Egypt* should have been on a collision course with, of all things, a steamer whose bows had been specially strengthened. Had the *Seine* been a normal vessel, the force of impact would have been reduced by her own bows buckling. But – no! Not she! She was built to bludgeon her way through pack ice, and it was perfectly possible for this much smaller ship to sink a much larger vessel such as the *Egypt* without coming to any harm. And why did the *Egypt* collide with the only vessel in the area in which the wireless transmitter was out of order? For, had the *Seine* been able to reply to the distress signals, the rescue operations might have been much better organized, and more lives might have been saved.

All this adds up to a very strange packet of coincidences, and one cannot help feeling that fate was in a most mysterious mood on that early evening in 1922.

8

The Ship that Changed her Shape

On a bright day in 1783, the East India Company's 300-ton sailing ship, *Antelope*, departed from the Chinese port of Macao, homeward bound for Britain. On board was a crew of fifty Europeans and sixteen Chinese. She was a graceful ship, armed with a battery of six-pounder guns to repel any pirates foolish enough to have designs on her cargo.

As she sailed out into the bay, a handful of onlookers waved their farewells to her crew. The morning sun seemed to accentuate the whiteness of her sails and the wake which creamed away from her stern as, gathering speed, she headed out into the South China Sea.

Presently the *Antelope* sailed out of sight, and the people on the quay went home.

Weeks and then months passed. No word came from the little sailing ship, and she was reported as overdue. By December, all hopes of ever seeing her again had been abandoned. She was added to the long list of vessels which had been lost without trace.

One afternoon, shortly before Christmas of that year, a man was walking along the waterfront at Macao. At some point, he stopped and looked out to sea. A vessel was approaching. Because he had nothing better to do, he sat down on a packing case and watched her draw closer.

As he managed to make out more details, he became aware that something was wrong with the ship. He asked himself what it was, but then found that he could not define it. You couldn't say that this was damaged, or that was missing, or anything else that was definite. It was just – well, just that she *looked* wrong.

Of course, he told himself, some naval architects were more clever than others, but whoever designed this vessel must have been a very bad one indeed. The proportions were all wrong. The masts were too short, and the hull – instead of being lean and beautiful – was ugly and stunted. And yet, the man scratched his head, there was something about her . . . something which was trying to come alive in his memory. It was as if he had seen her before, and yet had never seen her before. He frowned, and the ungainly vessel approached the quay.

The onlooker got up and strolled over to the wharf. A number of people had gathered round the strange ship which was now making fast. Suddenly there was an excited babble of conversation, and one man detached himself from the crowd, running for all he was worth in the direction of the East India Company's offices.

As he approached the stern of the ship, the onlooker could just make out her name. He quickened his pace, until he could read the letters. There it was, as plain as paint: ANTELOPE.

He stopped. This, surely, could not be the trim little sailing vessel which had vanished at sea all those months before? And nor, by all that was reasonable, could she have been any other member of her illustrious owners' fleet. They would never have accepted such a misshapen, hobbledehoy of the sea.

But, then again, there was this tiresome game that his memory was playing with him. Certain features were, admittedly, familiar. It was as if she were the *Antelope*, and as if she were not the *Antelope*. One might almost imagine that the ocean had performed some strange feat of magic on the ship, transforming her from an elegant vessel into a crude caricature of herself, in which most of the worst features were emphasized and most of the good ones removed.

Men were coming ashore from her. He did not know any of the *Antelope*'s crew personally, but his curiosity was now intense. Walking quickly, he elbowed his way through the spectators until he was able to grab the arm of a sailor.

'What has happened?' he asked. 'What is your ship? Who are you and where have you come from?'

The seaman smiled. 'That,' he said, 'is rather a long story.'

The better part of six weeks had passed since the *Antelope* had sailed from Macao. The winds had not been favourable, and she had made poor time. She was now, according to the reckoning of her master, Captain Wilson, somewhere in the area of the Malay archipelago.

On this particular night, there was an air of relaxation about the ship. According to the charts, there was no land for miles around; and, although there was enough wind to make about five knots with all sail set, the sea was not unpleasantly rough.

The officer of the watch paced across the quarterdeck, now and then checking the course on the compass, and occasionally peering upwards towards the spread of canvas. Down on the main deck, a small group of ratings were smoking their pipes and idly chatting.

And then, suddenly from the look-out: 'Breakers ahead!' Before the officer could give a change of course to the quartermaster, and before he could call the captain on deck, the *Antelope* was aground. Her keel crunched deep into sand. She leaned over at an alarming angle; and the sea was swirling around her, lashing at the side of the vessel with large waves.

To make matters worse, the weather was deteriorating. The moderate wind was working itself up into a gale. Some distance away, jabs of lightning and grumbles of thunder made it depressingly clear that they were in for a storm.

During one of these flashes, the mate thought he saw land ahead, but he could not be sure.

The *Antelope* seemed to be in no immediate danger of breaking up, but Captain Wilson was taking no chances. He told the men in the watch below to get dressed and be prepared to abandon ship. When they arrived on deck, every member of the crew was given a glass of wine and a biscuit.

To make sure that they could make a hurried departure, Wilson ordered one of the boats to be loaded with food and water, a compass, firearms, and ammunition. It was lowered carefully over the lee side, and moored in the shelter of the hull.

Meanwhile, an inspection below decks had revealed that the grounding had done a certain amount of damage to the planks. Water was coming in and threatening to damage the stock of provisions and ammunition. Laboriously, it was all carried up on deck and secured beneath tarpaulins.

By dawn, the storm had lessened. In the pale light they could see that they were stranded on what appeared to be a reef. About nine miles away, there was a small island; and, away over to the east, there were more islands.

'Right, Mr Berger,' the captain said to the first mate. 'I want you to take the two boats, and make for that island over there. See what you can find. If there are any natives, be polite. Try to be friendly with them. Don't use your guns except as a last resort.'

The mate and two boat crews departed.

Back on the *Antelope*, Captain Wilson became worried about the possibility of his ship breaking up. With the two boats now some distance away, the consequences would be disastrous for the men who remained on board. He called the carpenter over to him.

'I want you to take a party of men, and cut away the boom from the mizzen mast,' he said. 'Saw it up into suitable lengths, and make a raft out of it. It may be our only hope.'

The deck of the *Antelope* now became like a miniature shipyard. There was the thud of axes, the rasp of saws, and the rat-a-tat-tat of hammering. Presently, the raft began to take shape. It may not have been the ideal lifeboat, but it was strong, and the captain was well pleased with it.

While the carpenter and his helpers were putting the finishing touches to it, the two boats returned from the island. The mate reported that there was a good anchorage, plenty of fresh water, and there seemed to be no inhabitants.

Now began one of the most difficult parts of the whole operation. The raft was lowered over the side, loaded with stores and men, and taken in tow by the two boats.

They had not gone very far when somebody noticed that the carpenter was missing. It turned out that he had been busy packing up his tools, and had not noticed the sudden exodus. One of the boats went back for him.

The journey to the island was a rough one. The hardest part was that of crossing over the reef. The sea was seething furiously over the rocks, and it was only by lashing

'The journey to the island was a rough one . . .'

themselves to its timbers that the men on the raft avoided being washed overboard.

However, they made it. The island seemed to have been especially designed for castaways. It was everything that any writer of adventure stories has ever dreamed of – the kind of vision that Mr Roy Plumley must imagine every week, when he conducts *Desert Island Discs*. Indeed, when one thinks about it, one can almost hear that melody, compounded partly of lapping seawater and partly of seagull cries, that is so closely associated with yumyum trees, and coconut shells, and similar familiar images.

But, back in 1783, there was still a kind of novelty about such things, and the island was certainly real and no less evidently life-saving.

On the following day, they returned to the ship to bring off more supplies. The six-pounder swivel guns were among the items to be taken ashore. The island was certainly not inhabited, but there was land over to the east, which might very well be populated. And, as Captain Wilson pointed out, you never knew with natives. They might turn out to be as amiable as Santa Claus. On the other hand, they might very well be a bunch of bloodthirsty savages. If they were of the latter persuasion, a charge or two of honest British grapeshot would soon bring them to heel.

Also on board were several casks of brandy. The captain permitted one to be brought ashore, strictly for medical purposes. The remainder had to be destroyed. With a surprising zeal, which would have done credit to a federal agent during the American prohibition period, two seamen set about staving them in. It must have occurred to somebody that it was a waste of good brandy, but the captain's instructions were very clear on this point. The island was 'dry' when they first landed on it, and he intended things to stay that way.

Until now, there had been a faint hope that the sea would presently refloat the *Antelope*, and that it would be possible to repair her hull and sail her back to Macao. But the ocean appeared reluctant to carry out its side of the enterprise; and, in any case, a diversion occurred which needed rather more immediate attention.

Two canoes were approaching from the islands in the east. Each was manned by four natives. Six of them came ashore. They were tall men, naked, with copper-coloured skins that had been massaged repeatedly with coconut oil, and legs which were covered with elaborate patterns of tattoo marks from the ankles to the middle of the thighs. The men's hair was long and black, and rolled up neatly at the back, where it was tucked in close to the skull.

After the usual stuff about 'Me English!' and 'Parlez-vous Francais?' and 'Take me to your leader' and similar traditional British greetings to anyone who is obviously a foreigner, it transpired that the natives spoke Malay. One of the *Antelope*'s crew (a seaman named Tom Rose) could speak the language, and communications improved considerably. This was just as well; for the natives had never seen a white man before. They conceived the idea that these strange people, with their pallid skins and seafaring uniforms, were visitors from another planet (yes – really).

It was all very friendly. In the weeks to come, the sailors visited the natives on their islands, and the natives visited the crew of the *Antelope* on what had become, for want of anyone else to claim it, an outpost of the British Empire.

The only troublesome moment was when a party of canoeists broke into the wreck of the *Antelope* and drank the entire stock of medicine. It doesn't seem to have done them any good; but, which is no doubt more important, it didn't do them any harm either.

The high point in the relationship occurred when Captain Wilson introduced the islanders' king to the mystery of his six-pounders and other firearms. Delightedly dubbing them 'make thunders', the monarch was enthralled with their destructive possibilities, and asked whether he might borrow them for a war which he was waging against some other islands. Rather misguidedly, one might think, Captain Wilson said: 'Yes. And,' he added, 'you may have some of my sailors to fire them.'

From that moment, the war was a walkover. One can hardly consider it a triumph for the British virtue of sportmanship; but Captain Wilson would doubtless have justified his action by talking about 'bringing peace to the island'. It is the kind of fatuous utterance that statesmen have used throughout the ages, and will probably go on using far into the future.

Life on the desert island was becoming extremely tolerable, and there must have been some members of the *Antelope*'s crew who thought that it would be very nice to stay there for ever. But that is not quite what it is all about, and nobody understood this better than that austere old Scotsman, Captain Wilson. The ocean obviously did not intend to release *Antelope* from her bondage, and so some other plan would have to be devised.

The sheer optimism, the utter audacity of it, was remarkable. By now the *Antelope* was in pretty bad shape, and so the captain decided to take her to pieces, plank by plank, spar by spar, ladder by ladder, rope by rope, and, with these ingredients, to build another ship.

Trees were cut down on the island to serve as launching ways and blocks to support the hull. Under the direction of the carpenter, the crew worked for all they were worth and presently, after about six weeks, a new ship grew up on the slipway. She had a few of the features of her parent the *Antelope,* and many which were entirely alien. She looked like a travesty of the former sailing ship; but, which is the only thing that really matters in such a case, she *worked.*

One day in November, she was launched. Soon afterwards, with sails crammed on to her stubby spars and masts, she turned her back on the island and set off for Macao.

Her crew took with them the king's second son, Lee Boo, who was anxious to experience the delights of civilization. They left behind, as the white man's legacy, the jolly-boat and the rather less jolly six-pounder swivel guns.

And that is how the East India Company's sailing ship *Antelope* changed her shape. As the onlooker on the quayside at Macao remarked, when the sailor had told him the story, 'like most mysteries, it's perfectly simple, when you know the answer'.

9

The Man with a Pocketful of Fire

The convoy of merchant ships was spread out over the ink-dark surface of the North Atlantic. Destroyers, like dogs guarding a flock of elderly sheep, bounded about on the flanks. Everything looked peaceful enough, but nobody could be sure. For this was 1915, and the holds of the vessels were loaded with munitions from America for the Allied armies in Europe.

According to reliable reports, there were no German surface raiders in the vicinity, but that was the least of their worries. The real peril came from underwater, where the enemy U-boat fleet was deployed, silently stalking the convoy and intent upon catching some luckless merchantman unawares.

Suddenly, from an aged tramp steamer named *Phoebus*, a ragged column of smoke wriggled skywards. At first, there was nothing dramatic about it: no explosion, no sign that the ship was about to sink, none of the features associated with a U-boat attack.

Nevertheless, *Phoebus* was obviously in trouble. The smoke thickened, and flames could be seen licking her deck. One of the escort vessels hurried to her assistance.

The fire was eventually put out; but not before a consignment of ammunition intended for the Russian Army had been ruined. *Phoebus* herself was badly damaged. With a warship attending her, it was as much as she could do to limp in slow motion to Liverpool.

Phoebus' captain had no explanation to offer for the blaze. There had been no explosion: nothing even remotely resembling a torpedo attack. And he could think of nothing on board the ship which might have caused it. The cargo had been put on board at New York. The hatches had been battened down, and that was that.

Unless the German Navy had produced some new weapon, something which could penetrate a ship's hull without making a hole, the plight of the vessel could not be blamed on a U-boat. There had to have been some accident: some reasonably ordinary, logical, answer. But nobody could think what it was.

During the following months, several other such cases occurred. Certain features were common to them all. The fires always broke out in one or another of the holds. Sometimes the cargo was destroyed by the blaze; at others, it was ruined by the water used to put it out. Whichever it was, a valuable consignment of food or munitions was lost.

The ships themselves were seldom gutted by the fires, and loss of life was equally rare.

Reports on all the cases piled up on the desk of Admiral Sir Reginald Hall, Chief of Naval Intelligence in London. Studying them again and again, he detected a pattern, but it was incomplete. The key clue, which would point to the actual causes of the fires, was always missing. Just as a fish will eventually rise to a bait, he was sure that it would one day fall into his hands. The big problem was: would it come too late?

Captain von Rintelen of the Imperial German Navy was the very model of a gentleman. He was handsome, spoke several languages fluently, and had beautiful manners. He had also, which was more important to the German war effort, an extremely sharp and ingenious mind.

During the early days of the First World War, he served on the naval staff in Berlin. It was not a job that he particularly liked, for he would much rather have been in command of a ship at sea. However, there he was: his duties were not very arduous, and he had plenty of time in which to think.

In those days, the United States of America were neutral. As he studied the situation, however, it occurred to von Rintelen that there was something unpleasantly lopsided about it. That huge nation had an enormous output of arms and ammunition. Officially, anybody could buy them. But: you had to collect your purchases in your own ships.

The German merchant navy was in no position to take part in this shopping spree. A considerable number of its vessels were, indeed, stranded in American ports – unable to break through the screen of British naval ships which waited outside the territorial waters. And, even if they had been able to escape, it was highly unlikely that they would ever reach Germany's few ports. The result was that all the war materials were being sold to the Allies.

As von Rintelen thought more and more about it, his imagination got to work on a plan. Bearing a Swiss passport, he would take up residence in the United States – where, posing as an agent for the German Government, he would buy up all the nation's stocks of explosives. The fact that they could never be delivered didn't really matter. Purchase created ownership, and if the Germans cared to leave this portion of their property on American soil for the duration, that was their affair.

The German authorities approved of his idea. They gave him a Swiss passport plus two capsules containing a code. They were, he was assured, entirely digestible, and could be eaten if he ran into trouble.

He made the crossing to North America in a Norwegian liner, and presently took up residence in an hotel on New York's 57th Street. Before very long, he discovered that his original plan was out of the question – simply because the United States' output of gunpowder was so enormous that it would be quite impossible to buy up the entire market. However, by then, he had other things to occupy his attention.

One of the contacts he made early on during his stay in New York was a gentleman named Doctor Bunze. For some years, he had been the German consul in that city. Now he was employed as the Hamburg-American Line's representative.

One of Dr Bunze's achievements had been to load a number of freighters with coal and send them to sea. At some point on the ocean, they met up with German raiders and handed over their cargoes. Thus, the problem of refuelling was overcome, and the warships were able to continue their attacks on Allied shipping without any need to put back to Germany.

On waterfront matters Bunze was a mine of information. He knew all the German merchant marine officers and seamen, who were trapped in American ports, and fretting from lack of action. He was also acquainted with a number of Irishmen who (angry at Britain's slowness to give their country home rule) were hostile to the Allied cause. Doctor Bunze told von Rintelen about these things, and introduced him to German ships' captains and to Irish agitators. One day, he said, they might come in useful.

The day came soon enough. One morning, von

Rintelen was sitting in the small office that he had rented under the name of E. V. Gibbons, Inc. There was a knock on the door and a stranger came in. He introduced himself as Dr Scheele. He was, he explained, a chemist who was highly sympathetic to the German cause. As proof of his good intentions, he handed von Rintelen a letter from Captain von Papen, the military attaché in the United States.

Von Rintelen read the letter carefully. 'How can you help me?' he asked.

'It is difficult to explain,' Scheele said. 'It would be better if I were to show you.'

'I don't think I understand,' von Rintelen said.

'Please – it is better if I show you. I have an automobile outside. If you will just come on a short journey with me, you will see it all very clearly. It won't take long.'

The two men drove to a small wood about twenty miles outside the city. They left the car and walked a number of yards to a clearing in the trees.

'Now – watch,' Scheele said. 'It will not be many moments.'

Opening his briefcase, he took out a small metal tube, which he placed carefully on the ground.

'We had better stand back a little bit,' he said.

They waited for the better part of fifteen minutes; and then, suddenly, flames about ten inches long burst out from either end of the tube. For a few seconds, they burned brightly and intensely. Then they went out. There was no sign whatsoever of the tube.

'I call them my cigars,' Scheele said. 'You like them – eh?'

'Remarkable – quite remarkable,' von Rintelen said. 'Perhaps you'd like to tell me how it is done.'

The chemist explained that it was really quite simple.

You simply took a lead tube, and inserted a copper disc in the middle. Into one half of the tube, you poured sulphuric acid: into the other, picric acid. You then fitted each end with a wax plug and sealed it with a lead cap.

'What happens,' he said, 'is this. The sulphuric acid eats through the copper which is separating it from the picric acid. Once the two chemicals come into contact

'Suddenly flames about ten inches long burst out from either end of the tube'

with each other, they react vigorously and burst into flame. The flame is very hot, and melts the lead tube, leaving no traces. You can understand that the copper disc acts as a timing device. In other words, the thicker it is, the longer the sulphuric acid takes to burn through it.'

'Beautifully simple,' von Rintelen agreed, 'and not, I imagine, difficult to make.'

'Anyone could do it,' Scheele said.

Later, von Rintelen discussed the idea with his friend Dr Bunze. With a large force of unemployed German seamen only too eager to work for him, the application of Scheele's invention was simple. They would manufacture a large quantity of the incendiary 'cigars', and smuggle them into the holds of ammunition ships bound for Europe. The copper discs would be made to such a thickness, that they would burst into flames when the vessels were well out into the Atlantic.

There was only one problem: America was a neutral country, and it would be against international law to manufacture the devices on her territory. It is the kind of consideration which, nowadays, would mean nothing to a terrorist; but von Rintelen was a German officer first and a secret agent second. Whatever he did had to be done correctly.

Bunze had the answer. He pointed out that, among the German ships confined to American ports was a large liner named *Friedrich der Grosse*. This could quite reasonably be regarded as German territory, and it had the additional advantage of being right in the heart of dockland. The devices could be taken directly from the liner and planted in the holds of the ammunition ships.

To the delight of von Rintelen and to the consternation of Admiral Hall at British Naval Intelligence, the idea worked perfectly. A number of merchantmen went up in flames. Furthermore, since Scheele's incendiary 'cigars' destroyed themselves, there were no clues as to what had caused the fires.

No clues, that is to say, until a tramp steamer named

the *Kirk Oswald* set off on a voyage to the Russian port of Archangel.

The *Kirk Oswald* was heavily loaded with ammunitions, and, true to form, one of Scheele's inventions was smuggled aboard her. The copper disc was of such a thickness that the freighter would be well on her way to the Russian port before it went off.

When she was halfway across the Atlantic, however, her captain received an urgent signal. He was to alter course, and make for the French port of Marseilles instead. This meant a shorter trip – so much so, that the *Kirk Oswald* presently docked without any trouble at all, and with Scheele's device still lying in one of her holds.

The task of unloading the vessel began. Von Rintelen's secret might have remained undetected had it not been for an inquisitive stevedore. While he was working on board the ship, this man noticed a small metal object, shaped like a cigar and about four inches long lying at the bottom of a hold, Most people would either have ignored it, or else thrown it overboard. But the stevedore was curious. He wanted to know what it was, and he handed it, over to the French authorities.

It did not take them long to discover its purpose. When the news reached Admiral Hall, that gentleman heaved a colossal sigh of relief. The last piece of the jigsaw puzzle had fallen into place.

Franz von Rintelen was a popular figure in New York, and was reputed to be a successful businessman. But his contacts with the German and Irish elements in the American docks had not gone unnoticed. Admiral Hall already had a file on him.

The next round in this drama was in the best tradition of secret-service fiction. British agents in Washington employed a girl to become friendly with a young and rather badly paid secretary on the staff of the German Embassy. She managed to convince him that he could not live properly on his meagre salary; and that, in return for one simple action, he could make himself a small fortune.

'What is it?' he asked.

'You must make a copy of the Embassy's "most secret" code, and deliver it to me.'

'But,' he protested, 'it is always kept under lock and key.'

In Berlin, nobody under the rank of captain was allowed to handle a secret code; but, in Washington, things were not so strictly organized. It was quite common for secretaries to put away the codes after they had been used, and the girl knew this.

'Who has the key?' she asked.

'Well, ' he admitted, 'most of us do – at some time or another.'

'Very well,' she said. And: 'Can't you see – it is madness to go on living the way you do. Just this one little thing, and you could have so much happiness.'

The secretary went away from the meeting worried. On the one hand, there were shreds of German patriotism. On the other, an awareness that the girl had spoken the truth. He *was* badly paid. He *was* unhappy. And, after all, it was such a small thing to do. Presently, he had convinced himself that a trivial action, such as making a copy of the secret code, would not really damage the German war effort.

At that moment, the young man became a traitor and von Rintelen was doomed.

The young woman received the code, which was quickly relayed to Admiral Hall in London.

The discovery at Marseilles had put an end to von Rintelen's sabotage operations against Allied shipping.

He was now engaged in other schemes. One of them had to do with the smuggling of firearms to the rebels in Ireland. Another was the planning of a highly complex operation which, if it succeeded, would cause Mexico (with German support, of course) to go to war against the United States.

On the morning of June 6th, 1915, he was having breakfast in the New York Yacht Club, when one of the servants brought him a message. He had to telephone the German Naval Attaché. The outcome of the conversation was that he left the club immediately, and walked to a certain street corner, where the Attaché was waiting for him.

No words were spoken. Von Rintelen was simply handed a slip of paper. On it was written: 'To the Naval Attaché at the Embassy. Captain Rintelen is to be informed unobtrusively that he is under instructions to return to Germany.'

He booked a passage on the Dutch liner, *Noordam.*

The voyage back to Europe passed without any incident until the ship reached Dover. During the First World War, as part of the British blockade of Germany, all neutral ships were stopped off the Kent port and boarded by contraband control officials.

This was the moment that Admiral Hall had been waiting for. As soon as the secret code had come into his possession, he had got busy preparing the trap. It was he who had sent the message recalling von Rintelen to Germany. After that, he merely had to ensure that all neutral ships were thoroughly searched, and that particular attention was paid to their lists of passengers.

During his stay in New York, von Rintelen had traded under the name of E. V. Gibbons, Inc. For his voyage back to Europe, he had decided to use the same initials, and to call himself E. V. Gaché. He was, he told people, a Swiss who, at one time, had been attached to that country's legation in Berlin.

It was a brave attempt to deceive, but it did not succeed. At seven o'clock one morning, he was taking a bath. A few minutes earlier, he had heard the jingle of the engine-room telegraph, and the vibrations of the ship's engines had stopped. Through the bathroom porthole he could see the white cliffs of England. In his imagination he saw a launch coming alongside, and the contraband men climbing up the ladder. The date was Friday, August 13th. He hoped, fervently, that there was nothing significant about it.

He did not have long to wait. As he was lying in the warm water there was a knock at the door.

'What is it?' He called.

'Some British naval officers wish to have a word with you,' the steward said.

Von Rintelen dried himself and got dressed. On deck, he found two officers and ten sailors with fixed bayonets waiting for him.

'You are Mr Gaché?' one of the officers asked.

'Yes.'

'We have orders to take you with us.'

Thus, on a warm summer's morning off Dover, von Rintelen's story came to an end. He had played his role as a secret agent carefully. When in New York he had seldom made any move without, first of all, consulting a corrupt lawyer whom he retained. Because America had not yet entered the war, and because his operations had all taken place on neutral territory, it was impossible to convict him as a spy. It was this careful regard for the letter of the law which saved von Rintelen's life.

Nevertheless, it did not protect his freedom. After intensive cross-examination, he was interned in Derbyshire for the next two years. In 1917, the United States, which by then had joined forces with the Allies, applied for his extradition to face a charge of sabotage. He returned to New York in the White Star liner *Adriatic*; was tried by an American court and sentenced to four years' imprisonment. It was not until 1921 that the man who had done so much damage to Allied shipping finally went home to Germany.

10

The Trouble with Iron

Ships had always been built of wood, and their power had come from the wind. But then, in the middle of the nineteenth century, the ironmasters stalked on to the scene in their stove-pipe top hats and their frockcoats and their side-whiskers. With the ironmasters came the steam-engine builders, and the paddle-wheel makers, and the men who said: 'Ah – yes. A paddle steamer is all very fine, but you would do better with a *screw*.'

These men were the prophets of a new kind of vessel. The ironmasters explained that their ships would be *stronger*. The engineers said: 'Consider the wind. It is all very well to depend upon it, but is it *reliable*? Sometimes it blows in the wrong direction. Sometimes it blows too hard. Sometimes it doesn't blow at all.' And sailors remembered times when they had been becalmed for days on end, and they said: 'Ah, yes. Well – possibly.'

Gradually people began to take the ideas of these men seriously. They saw that iron ships might, indeed, be better than wooden ones; and they realized that, providing they worked, steam engines would free them from the uncertain ways of the wind. It was a glorious thought that, quite possibly, they might be able to set out on a voyage, and have a reasonably accurate idea of when they would reach the other end.

In this age of innovation, inventors had a wonderful time. When they were successful, everyone marvelled at them. Even those who said 'It will never work' (and there were plenty of them) had to take back their words.

But every new invention was a mystery. If it came out right the first time, there was nothing more to worry about. But if it failed, the mystery deepened. If you could discover what had gone wrong, it could be corrected. But it was seldom so easy.

This would have been all very well, if failure had merely meant that the inventor had to think again. Unfortunately, when the object in question was a ship, a mistake usually cost lives.

There was, for example, the case of HMS *Captain*, which came to grief one stormy night in 1870. She was the dream ship of a naval captain who had taken part in the Crimean War. During the attack on the Russian forts at Sebastopol, he had decided that the best type of man-of-war would be a raft with a gun mounted on it. By no means the least of its advantages would be that it would present a much smaller target to the enemy.

He lived with this idea for a long time, and presently designed a ship which put the essence of it into practice. The vessel in question was to be powered by steam engines driving two propellers, and was to have an exceptionally low freeboard*. As a concession to general opinion, the poop and the fo'c'sle were to be built along more conventional lines, but the main deck would only be eight feet above the water.

In designing his vessel he had to take into account the fact that, in those days, there was no such thing as the perfect steam engine. Large quantities of coal had to be carried; and, even so, there was always the possibility that it might break down. Consequently, the early steamers were rather like a man who insists on wearing braces as

* The distance between the waterline and the deck.

well as a belt. They had their engines to be sure, but they were also rigged as sailing ships.

That was to be the downfall of HMS *Captain*, which was the name of this unusual vessel. On top of a hull which, when guns were mounted on it, had only marginally more freeboard than a yacht, there were three tall masts and enough sail to drive a fully-rigged ship. A number of experts expressed doubts about the idea, and they were right. It was entirely lacking in stability.

During her early voyages one or two people remarked that the trouble with *Captain* was 'she didn't roll easily', and that she was a 'stiff ship'. From a gunner's point of view, this was excellent. It meant that he had a steady platform from which to fire. But seamen, who understood these things, were not nearly so happy about it. They knew that a vessel which rolls heavily may be uncomfortable, but she is unlikely to turn turtle.

One night in 1870, HMS *Captain* was returning to Britain from Gibraltar in company with other warships. The wind got up to very nearly gale force, and the other vessels took in sail. But H. T. Burgoyne, VC, *Captain*'s commanding officer, was either foolish, or else had immense confidence in his ship (which as time was to show, amounted to much the same thing). He refused to do anything about it; kept the fires in his boilers banked, his engines at 'Stop', and flew on before the gale as if taking part in a race.

Just before midnight, the wind increased to gale force and the ship heeled over to an alarming degree. Captain Burgoyne, who was taking it easy in his cabin, was called up on to the bridge. He saw what was wrong at once, but it was too late. No sooner had he given orders to bring in the sails, than *Captain* capsized. Only 18 of the 500 men on board her survived.

During her brief life (she was completed in 1869), HMS *Captain* had become a popular ship, and all but a few experts at the Admiralty had eventually overcome their doubts about her design. After the disaster there were plenty of people who were only too eager to say that they had known it would happen.

Nevertheless, there was one man to whom the loss of HMS *Captain* would always have been a mystery, and that was Captain C. P. Coles, RN (Retired), the ill-fated ship's designer. But Captain Coles was in no position to worry about anything at all. He was one of the 482 who went down in her.

HMS *Captain* was a freak. She should never have been built. Her Majesty's troopship, *Birkenhead*, was a very different matter. There was nothing whatsoever wrong with her design. She behaved herself well in a rough sea and, according to a writer in *The Times*, 'her performance proves her to have been the fastest, most carrying and comfortable vessel in Her Majesty's service as a troopship, and one that can be fully relied on in hull and machinery'. If *The Times* said that, it meant it.

And yet, one night in 1852, the *Birkenhead* went aground on a rock one mile off the South African coast. The disaster has become a classic example of heroism: of the 638 souls on board, 445 perished. According to the legend, many of the soldiers went down standing to attention in drill formation. It makes an impressive story, and it is probably true. But the really interesting thing about the *Birkenhead*, the mystery which has been a continual source of argument over the years, is *why*, exactly, she struck the rock.

Would it have happened if she had *not* been an iron ship?

'. . . the soldiers went down standing to attention in drill formation'

According to a court of inquiry which followed the tragedy, most of the blame could be attributed to her captain, Master Commander Robert Salmond, RN. It was alleged that, in an attempt to save time, he set a course too close to the shore.

Outside official circles, however, there were a number of intelligent people who were anxious to clear Mr Salmond's name. They suggested that he may not have been at fault at all. The mistake, they argued, which caused the total destruction of this fine troopship, was not made by any human being. It was created by the compass.

The *Birkenhead* had sailed from Cork on January 7th, 1852, bound for the naval base at Simonstown – a few miles to the east of Cape Town. The troops on board her were urgently needed reinforcements for Army units fighting a war against the Kaffirs. Some of them had their wives and children with them.

For the first ten days of her voyage, the *Birkenhead* had to battle against gale-force winds and heavy seas. Most of the people on board were extremely ill. But, by and by, the weather improved, and she made Simonstown in forty-seven days, which included stops at Madeira, Sierra Leone and St Helena. This was extremely good. Her shortest time for the passage to Cape Town had been forty-four days compared with fifty-six days for the only vessel with an even remotely comparable speed.

At the naval base, there was a crisis. The reinforcements were desperately needed up at the front. The captain was told to take on coal and proceed to sea as quickly as possible. A number of horses were added to the ship's passenger list, and they were quartered on the main deck.

By six o'clock on the evening of February 25th, the *Birkenhead* was ready to sail once more. Her voyage was to take her 500 miles, right round the Cape of Good Hope to a place called Algoa Bay (on the modern atlas it is very close to Port Elizabeth). There the soldiers and the horses were to disembark, and move up country to the war.

It was a beautiful night, with a perfectly clear sky, no wind and only a gentle swell to disturb the otherwise placid sea. *Birkenhead* steamed on her way with her sails furled, and the splash and thump of her paddle wheels serenading her progress. Over to port, the dim shape of land could just be made out.

At nine o'clock, most of the soldiers turned in, and at midnight the watch on deck changed. The departing helmsman passed on the course to his relief. 'South south-east half east,' he said. Master Commander Salmond was lying on his bunk, with his frockcoat off and a dressing-gown on, fitfully dozing.

The ship was doing seven and a half knots.

If Salmond was resting, he cannot have been in any doubts about the position of his ship. He was an extremely experienced seaman with a good record. Nevertheless, when one of the Army officers, who was up on deck enjoying the calm of the night, asked the officer of the watch for their position, he received a surprise. It happened that the soldier knew this section of the coast very well, and he was interested in the identity of a cluster of lights ashore. According to his reckoning, they should have been in the vicinity of a headland named Danger Point.

But: 'No,' the ship's officer said. 'I don't believe you're right. I estimate they are on Agulhas Point.'

If, and it is possible, the Army officer was right and the sailor was wrong, it meant that *Birkenhead* was eighty miles off course.

At two o'clock in the morning, the troopship struck the rock. The force of the impact threw the look-outs off their feet, and there was a fearful noise as her paddle wheels drove her relentlessly forward, and the rough surface of the ledge prised her iron plates apart and forced out the rivets. Slowly, abjectly, the fine vessel tilted over to starboard.

Master Commander Salmond, still wearing his dressing-gown, was up on deck in an instant. He ordered the engines to be stopped, and then went forward to examine the damage.

Meanwhile the first hysteria of panic was affecting the horses, the women and children, and, to some extent, the troops. The horses were dealt with by the simple expedient of cutting them loose and pushing them overboard. In theory, they ought to have been able to swim to the shore, which was only about a mile away. In fact, the surrounding waters were infested with sharks, which attacked the unfortunate animals and devoured a number of them.

There was nothing much to be done about the women and children for the moment; but Major Alexander Seton, who was in command of the military, soon had the soldiers under control. It was a magnificent example of Army discipline at its best. One moment, they were a rabble of disorganized, badly frightened men. The next, they were calm, orderly, and supremely confident in their commanding officer to get them out of whatever mess the *Birkenhead* had landed them in.

Salmond, who had now returned to the quarterdeck, had to make an intolerably difficult decision. He could either leave his ship where she was, and run the risk of her being broken up by the waves. Or, he could put the engines astern, back her off, and hope that she still had enough buoyancy to remain afloat until everyone had been safely taken off in the boats.

He chose the latter course. As things turned out, it was probably the wrong one. The ordeal of being wrenched off the surface of the rock did still more damage to the hull, and caused the engine room to be flooded. However, two of the boats were lowered, and the women and children embarked in them.

All the time, the *Birkenhead* was steadily sinking by the stern. About twenty minutes after striking the rock, she broke in two. The horror was indescribable. The foremast snapped close to the deck and came crashing down. The tall, thin funnel was jolted loose and smashed down on one of the paddle boxes, utterly destroying most of the remaining boats. There was a litter of broken spars and twisted rigging everywhere, and yet still Master Commander Salmond and Major Seton remained calm, and still the troops stood fast.

Clearly, the *Birkenhead* had not many more minutes, or even seconds to live. The temptation to abandon ship in a free-for-all must have been tremendous. But Major Seton realized that, if hundreds of men were suddenly turned loose into the water, the danger to the women and children in the boats would have been considerable.

And so the men stood fast, and the *Birkenhead* sank, and there was a great collection of debris and men scattered all over the sea. Of the great troopship, the fastest vessel on the run from Britain to South Africa, only the mainmast remained. It stuck out of the water, with survivors clinging on to it; but, already, it had the appearance of a ghoulish grave to the vanquished ship and her doomed soldiers and sailors.

Some men managed to struggle to the shore. Many drowned or were eaten by sharks trying to get there. Even more perished at the scene of the wreck. And the world was left to consider the question of why did the *Birkenhead* strike the rock.

Was it an error by her captain, or did her compass lie?

A compass is a magnetic instrument. It is bound to be affected by metal. In 1804, a frigate named *Apollo* was escorting a convoy of thirty-six merchant ships to the Mediterranean. She went ashore on the coast of Portugal, and many of the merchant ships suffered the same fate. A great many lives were lost. The investigation which followed the disaster put the blame on iron fittings installed near the *Apollo*'s compass. They had, the court of inquiry said, caused it to give a false reading.

December 1811: the warship *Defence* went aground on the coast of Jutland. Five hundred and eighty-seven lives were lost. Verdict: compass error brought about by the vessel's iron guns and fittings.

One of the men who had fought with great determination for the future of the iron ship was a tall Scotsman whose father had founded a shipyard at Birkenhead. His name was John Laird.

Laird realized that, if he were to sell iron ships, the problem of false compass readings would have to be overcome. In 1834, he invited Professor G. P. Airey, the Astronomer Royal, to carry out a number of tests aboard a steamer named the *Rainbow*, which had been built in his yard.

As a result of this work, Airey gave it out that, since an iron ship was iron all over, it had a different effect from that of a moveable object on board a wooden ship. It certainly pulled the compass off course, but the misdirection was constant. If you discovered what it was, you could correct it.

The state of the art improved. By the time the *Birkenhead* was commissioned, it was generally considered that the problem had been overcome. Nevertheless, in the months which followed the investigation into the wreck, a number of points came to light.

One took the form of a letter to a newspaper, in which the correspondent pointed out that the *Birkenhead*'s compass was *known* to be unreliable. On one occasion, he asserted, the ship had been swung round three times in a complete circle off Spithead. And yet, during these manoeuvres, the compass had never moved.

He also alleged that once, when the *Birkenhead* was out at sea, the iron produced such a chaotic effect on the compasses, that the captain had to take them up to one of the mastheads, and navigate the ship from there.

But suppose the writer of this letter was one of those eccentric characters who sometimes burst into print. Suppose his case against the *Birkenhead*'s compass depended on two stories, both of which were false.

The ship was obviously off course when she struck the rock, and yet it seems unlikely that Master Commander Robert Salmond would have made such a blunder. Is there any possibility that conditions that night were such that the *Birkenhead*'s compass, normally (let us say) reliable, was rendered inaccurate?

A report from Cape Town suggested that there was. Although it was a calm, almost beautiful, night, the weather had been unsettled, and there was a lot of electricity in the atmosphere. A number of ships were anchored in Table Bay, and several of the captains reported that their compasses were giving unreliable readings. Furthermore, the master of a Royal Mail steamer announced that his had suddenly swung round from east to south-west.

Finally, when Thomas Coffin, the man who had been at the wheel at the time of the disaster, was asked: 'Was the compass sluggish or not?', he replied: 'Rather slow in moving'.

The evidence for Master Commander Salmond and against the *Birkenhead*'s compass may not have been overwhelming, but it was certainly enough to throw a good deal of suspicion on the latter. According to British law, a man is innocent unless it can be proved beyond any reasonable doubt that he is guilty. With the possibility of a traitor lurking in his binnacle, it cannot be said that the case against Salmond was strong enough to find him at fault. Not, indeed, that it mattered very much to him, poor man – for he went down with his ship.

11

The Ghost of a Battleship

A mystery remains a mystery until somebody discovers an explanation. A detective story is only a mystery until the plot is unravelled in the last chapter. And, even then, it is not a complete mystery; for, all the time, somebody (the villain) knows what has actually happened.

The only time that something is totally mystifying is when all the evidence has been removed, and when nobody is left alive to tell the story. The case of the *Mary Celeste* falls into this category, and so does the episode of the *Ellen Austin* and the schooner which disappeared with several members of her crew.

But such instances are very rare indeed. Far more common are situations in which one man is puzzled and another man is doing the puzzling. For example, the head of British Naval Intelligence was perplexed by the mysterious fires which broke out in Allied merchantmen during 1915. Captain von Rintelen, on the other hand, was not – for it was he who caused them. It was a battle of wits, with one man knowing the answers, and the other trying to find them.

Perhaps the world is divided into the mystifiers and the mystified, and whether there is a mystery or not depends upon which of the two you belong to.

For example:

An American couple were on their way home to the United States in October 1914 – two months after war had broken out. They were travelling in the giant White Star liner, *Olympic*, and they boarded her at Liverpool. On the first day out, they passed the coast of Northern Ireland round about noon. They took lunch, and went on deck afterwards. There was, they noticed, an unusually large number of people gathered at the forward end of the ship. They joined them.

'What's happening?' the man asked.

'Look over there,' he was told. 'There's a battleship in trouble.'

Sure enough, wallowing in the sea ahead, with her stern well down in the water, was a large British man-of-war. A cruiser and a number of destroyers were standing by her, ready, it appeared, to take off survivors.

'Must have been torpedoed by a German submarine,' somebody said.

What the spectators did not know was that the battleship had struck a mine, and that her distress signal had been picked up by the *Olympic*'s radio operator. The liner's master, Captain H. J. Haddock, had altered course to see whether he could be of any help to the stricken ship.

During the next hour or so, the excitement on board the liner became intense. In a brave effort which, had it come off, would have made naval history, Captain Haddock tried to take the battleship in tow. One attempt followed another, and, each, time, the hawser snapped. Finally, at four o'clock in the afternoon, Captain Haddock was compelled to give up.

However, he continued to stand by the mortally wounded warship, and presently some of her crew were transferred to the liner. The passengers gathered eagerly round them.

'What ship are you from?' they asked.

'HMS *Audacious*,' the sailors told them. They said that they had been out on a gunnery exercise with two other battleships. Shortly after discharging their guns at the target, there had been a huge explosion. Within a matter of seconds, *Audacious* had begun to settle by the stern; but, even so, she had managed to struggle towards home

'Captain Haddock tried to take the battleship in tow . . .'

at nine knots for nearly two hours, before her pumps became unable to cope with the inrush of water. The hopes of getting *Audacious* back to her base at Lough Swilly in North West Ireland had obviously become very slender indeed; and, in fact, she finally sank at nine o'clock that night.

Like most of the other passengers, the couple took snapshots of the crippled battleship and the attempts to take her in tow.

After the war, they made another trip to Britain. In one of the hotels at which they stayed, they met a Scotsman, and the American described the encounter with the battleship.

'Her name was *Audacious*,' he said. 'I guess she sank later that day – there can't have been any hope for her. Here: I have a photo I took of her.'

Taking out his wallet, he showed his companion a snapshot of the situation, just after the *Olympic*'s towrope had parted for the last time.

The Scotsman looked at it carefully. 'I agree,' he said. 'You'd never imagine that they could have got her back, but they must have done. HMS *Audacious* – I remember her quite well. We often used to see her in Loch Ewe, and a friend of mine who was in the Navy came across her in Scapa Flow on a number of occasions.'

Both men were mystified. Here was a snapshot which showed a vessel that was obviously sinking, and which it had been impossible to take in tow. And here was a man who had seen her on a number of occasions *after* the episode.

If ships had ghosts, that would certainly have been the answer. But they do not; and, in any case, the man-of-war which the Scotsman had seen, and which he identified as HMS *Audacious*, had nothing to do with the supernatural. It was an extremely cunning hoax.

The loss of HMS *Audacious* occurred at an embarrassing time for the British Government. On the one hand, they wanted to convince the Germans that the Royal Navy was vastly superior to the Imperial German Navy; and, on the other, they wished to create an impression of absolute power to the Turks, who were showing disturbing signs of being about to enter into an alliance with Germany.

As Winston Churchill, who was then First Lord of the Admiralty, said: the loss of a major British capital ship such as *Audacious* would have done the nation's prestige a great deal of harm.

And so, with considerable ingenuity, they decided to keep her alive.

An eighteen-year-old Canadian Pacific liner named the *Montcalm* was requisitioned for the purpose. Using large quantities of wood, paint, and canvas, she was transformed into a very passable likeness of the lost battleship. Then she was taken up to Loch Ewe in the North West of Scotland, where she spent most of her time at anchor. Now and again, she was let out on trips to Scapa Flow.

The important thing was that the Germans should know of her presence, and yet never be allowed to bring her to action. The deception worked very well until the end of 1915, when the trappings of the masquerade were stripped off, and the *Montcalm* was converted into a fleet oil tanker.

Of all the people who had been on board the *Olympic* that afternoon, only one knew the full story of the *Audacious* and the impostor. And that was Captain Haddock. After his trip to New York, he joined the Royal Navy, and promptly took command of the project responsible for the fake battleship.

Piccolo non-fiction

Piccolo All the Year Round Book 50p
Deborah Manley

Collecting Things 30p
Elizabeth Gundrey

Amazing Scientific Facts 25p
Jane Sharman

A Diary of Yesterdays (illus) 45p
Tony Bastable

Great Polar Adventures (illus) 40p
Marie Herbert

Piccolo Encyclopedia of Sport 50p
Peter Mathews

Piccolo Encyclopedia of Useful Facts 50p
Jean Stroud